First Print Edition 2011

Copyright by Z-Hat Custom Inc.

432 E. Idaho St.

Suite C420

Kalispell, MT 59901

Library of Congress Control Number: 2010942652

ISBN # 978-0-9831598-03

ALWAYS WERE SAFETY GLASSES AND HEARING
PROTECTION WHEN RELOADING OR SHOOTING.

If you are unfamiliar with the terminology and processes
described here you are responsible to learn more. Do research,
understand terminology, and think; your brain is the best safety
device available.

The author and publishers of this book are not responsible for the
use or misuse of it's contents by any individual or group. Utilize
safe loading practices. Always start low and work up loads. Just
because the loads published here were safe in test guns does not
mean they will be safe in any other gun.

TE DUE

Reloading Manual

Edited by Fred Zeglin

Table of Contents

Authors Note

Originally this text was produced as an E-Book and distributed on CD. Over the years I have received many requests for a print edition; so, here it is.

Hawk Cartridges have proven to have staying power. Many years have passed since Dave Scovill wrote about the 375 Hawk/Scovill and I introduced the rest of the Hawk line. These cartridges were featured in later Wayne van Zwoll articles. Clients still request chambering for them on a regular basis. Some cartridges in the line receive more attention than others, and rightly so.

This collection of data includes some new material and new cartridges that were not included in the electronic version of the manual. The intention is to provide information that time has shown to be valuable to shooters of Hawk Cartridges.

I also wanted to take this opportunity to thank all the clients who have utilized my services over the years as a result of the attention that Hawk Cartridges brought my way. Your business has been, and is, much appreciated.

Fred Zeglin

Acknowledgments

Gathering data for a book like this requires a lot of resources, it cannot be done without the assistance of others. Many friends and businesses contributed freely of time and materials to help make a Hawk Cartridges Reloading Manual possible. Listed in no particular order:

Mike Brady, founder of North Fork Bullets

Greg Mushial of GMDR (RCBS.Load)

Keith Anderson, Western Powders

Accuracy Powders

Kaltron-Pettibone

Cris Hodgdon, Hodgdon Powders

Andy Hill, Hawk Bullets

Pete Cardona, Quality Cartridge

Sierra Bullets

Graydon Snapp

Steve Wright

Bruce Nichols, Mountain Sun Photo

Ken Kempa

Swift Bullets

Michael Petrov

Dave Kiff, Pacific Tool & Gage

Dave Scovill, Wolfe Publishing

Wayne van Zwoll

Mike Thomas

Doug Gregory

Dick Williams

Chris Carlson

Alvin Byars

Ed Reynolds

Recreational Software Inc. (Pressure Trace)

There are probably a hundred more people who deserve to be here, please forgive me. I have a photographic memory but it's pre-digital and film seems to be scarce these days.

Foreword

Fred and I met at a pivotal time and place for the both of us. The time was 1996 and the place was in the shop of Bob Fulton. Bob was the designer of the concept of the Hawk cartridge with the debut of the 375 Hawk with the 411 Hawk to follow. With Bob's blessing, Fred was going to begin offering custom rifles chambered in Hawk cartridges as well as expand the concept over a far wider range of calibers. Also at this time, I was exploring a new career as I was tired of traveling overseas with my, at that time, petro-chemical job.

Bob had an idea of a new bullet design and after some discussions I decided to take that idea and see what I could do with it. That was the birth of North Fork Technologies. It was my opinion that one could not state for certainty the performance of such a product without pressure testing. I purchased an Oehler M43 to pressure test my product in various cartridges.

I was always impressed with the Hawk cartridges and there began the symbiotic relationship between Fred and I and North Fork and Hawk Cartridges. I needed to test bullets and Fred needed pressure data for his expanding line of cases. Fred and I spent many a long day at the range taking up three benches with computers, guns, and reloading equipment gathering data for the both of us, not to mention the data gathered at my shop on the indoor range.

It was an enlightening period of my life as we both learned the nuances of our endeavors. Over the course, we learned that some "truths" that had been repeated over and over were, in fact, not true and also that some of the ideas of those that went before us were good as gold. Although I was only involved with the original line of cartridges that Fred developed, Fred soon purchased his own pressure equipment and went on to gather data for his whole line.

Hopefully you will enjoy the data presented here on the most efficient line of cartridges ever developed as much as I enjoyed spending time gathering that data with my friend, Fred Zeglin.

Mike Brady

North Fork Tech (originator)

Part I

How it all started!

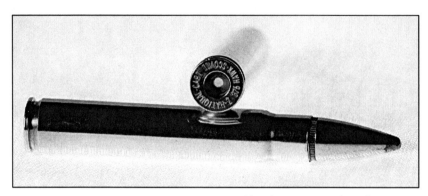

Photo by www.mountainsunphotoart.com

It was in the latter part of 1988 when Bob Fulton, designer of renowned HAWK Bullets, had the idea to build rifle that was suitable for dangerous game, as well as anything in North American. Recoil was another major factor, Bob wanted an 8 pound rifle that would not beat him up. A friend gave Bob a rifle chambered in 375 Whelen Improved. Bob was not impressed with the mediocre ballistics. So he started looking for a better cartridge design, based on the 30-06 case, since he was too cheap to buy a new barrel.

With Bob's long background in guns he had seen and shot many wildcats. He was aware of the Gibbs line of cartridges, but the goal was not to wring every last foot per second out of the 06 case. Rather, to have a reliable feeder and make the most efficient use of it. Considerations of the design were weight, cost, brass availability, low cost brass, low recoil and muzzle blast, and easy conversion of any 06 size action. Bob wanted a case that is easy to form as well.

So Bob decided to use the basic design of the 9.3x62 (often called the 30-06 or Africa) not being a gunsmith he just jammed the reamer into the chamber until he liked what he saw. The effect was a case with the shoulder moved forward and a straighter body taper than the 06. Bob managed to increase the powder capacity of the venerable old 30-06 cartridge by a total of 9% over the original design. He used the original 17 degree shoulder angle to facilitate reliable feeding. At the same time he retained a useful neck length of .329". Knowledgeable wildcatters use about 90% of caliber as a neck length for good neck tension and overall accuracy.

375 Whelen Ackley Imp.

Editors note: *Depending on which resource you check the 9.3x62 is listed with both a 17 degree and a 25 degree shoulder.*

When Bob went to the range with is new gun and a chronograph he was pleasantly surprised. His original goal was to increase velocity to 2600 fps with a 250 gr. bullet. The old coot discovered that he could easily surpass his original goal with a wide margin for safety. In reality he achieved 2700 fps with a 250gr. bullet.

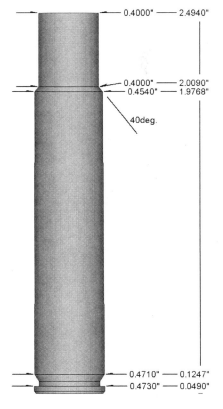

[Case Cap. 77.27 gr.]

Bob paid a visit to Dave Scovill at Wolfe Publishing in 1991, they print "Rifle" & "Handloader" magazines. He sat a 375 Whelen Improved and a 375 Hawk cartridge on Dave's desk. Like most wildcats, seeing is more impressive than hearing.

The way Bob tells it, "Scovill was favorably impressed with what he saw." Dave scooped up the cartridges and an article was underway.

Dave borrowed the original rifle from Bob for some time. Bob's favorite loads for the 375 Hawk were all with H4895 which was formulated for use in the 06 case. It was Dave's contention that with modern powders we should get even better results. Dave also had two guns of his own built in 375 Hawk in order to fully test the cartridge.

9.3x62mm Mauser

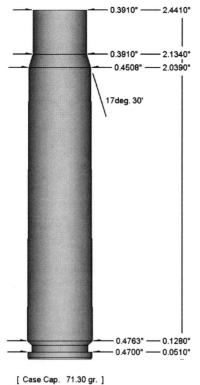

0.3910" — 2.4410"

0.3910" — 2.1340"
0.4508" — 2.0390"

17deg. 30'

0.4763" — 0.1280"
0.4700" — 0.0510"

[Case Cap. 71.30 gr.]

In 1993 Dave Scovill published an article in Handloader #166 titled, ".375 Hawk/Scovill." Dave chose to convert the Hawk dimensions from those used on the 9.3x62 to the more common 30-06 base dimensions. When Bill Keyes of RCBS made the dies for Dave he took the liberty of making the name change to "Hawk/Scovill". Dave stated in his article that the changes had no effect on ballistics whatsoever.

Bob had always used 30-06 brass for his 375 Hawk with no difficulty. The difference in dimensions serves an important purpose Bob explains, "The 9.3x62 follows the standard British practice of slightly looser chambering for use in Africa and other hot climates. That improves reliability of extraction, the extra room in the chamber is there to take advantage of the way that brass stretches and contracts." Dave noted that this left a slight bulge on the case at the web, he cited concerns about stretching and possible head separations as the reason for using the smaller 06 case dimensions for his version of the 375 Hawk. Ballistically the two versions are identical although ammunition cannot be interchanged.

Scovill tested a wide variety of bullets and powders in an effort to get the most out of the 375 Hawk/Scovill. No matter what he did including having two rifles chambered for the Hawk/Scovill design he never really equaled Bob's original rifle ballistically. Scovill's approach seemed to be more oriented toward light bullets for caliber and max velocity, while Fred was content with a 250 grain bullet at 2700 fps.

Dave Scovill also pointed out that, "Bullet weights from 210 to 300 grains shot to approximately the same point of aim. On one afternoon 55 shots were fired with a selection of loads and bullets weighing from 220 to 300 grains using the same aiming point on the target. The resultant group measured 3.6 inches." This was at 100 yards.

Experience with the 375 Hawk/Scovill indicates that it performs it's very best with 235gr. and 250gr. bullets and H4895. Case life is very good with moderate loads, which is probably one of the best measures of safe pressures.

Simply put, the 375 Hawk will easily match the trajectory of a 30-06, 180gr. bullet at 2700 fps. The important difference is that the 375 Hawk does it with a 250gr. bullet. A 30-06 with a 180gr. bullet has a point blank range of 268.1 yards (that is, point and shoot), the 375 Hawk with a 250gr bullet has a point blank range of 264.7 yards. Of course more important than that is the energy delivered, with a muzzle velocity of 2700 fps the 06 delivers 2913 foot pounds at the muzzle, while the 375 Hawk delivers 4046 foot pounds (more than two tons!).

Where did all the other Hawk calibers come from?

In 1995 Graydon Snapp walked into Fred Zeglin's Shop in Casper, Wyoming, Sandbar Gunsmithing. Graydon had read the article about the 375 Hawk. Being a fan of the 35 Whelen he was sure that a 358 Hawk would be the way to go. Graydon had even written to Dave Scovill to ask about the idea. Since Bob Fulton lived just 25 miles away Graydon had also looked him up and introduced Fred and Bob.

Reamers are expensive, so running out and buying a 358 Hawk reamer was something that both Fred and Graydon hesitated over. Fred had the opportunity to pick up a 375 Hawk/Scovill chamber reamer on sale from Clymer Mfg. He talked it over with Graydon and ordered the reamer. When the 375 Hawk was

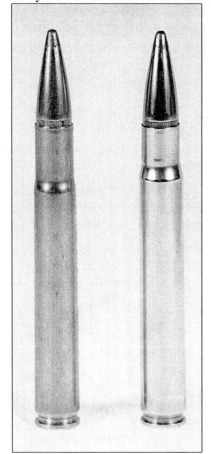

finished range testing was the first order of business. Pleasantly enough, Fred found that the rifle would reproduce the results in the Handloader article nearly perfectly.

Left: *375 Whelen vs. 375 Hawk.*
Photo by www.mountainsunphotoart.com

Graydon was so pleased with the results of his new 375 that he decided the 358 Hawk (his first choice) was now a must. At the same time Fred was so impressed with the results of the 375 Hawk that he decided to build a 338 Hawk. Fred ordered the reamers in September of 1996.

Fred's personal rifle wears a 23-inch Shilen barrel in 338 Hawk. It produced this set of data:

225 gr. Hornady, H-4895 55.0 gr. 2726 feet per second (fps)

225 gr. Hornady, H-335 53.0 gr. 2623 fps

225 gr. Speer, IMR-4064 55.5 gr. 2592 fps

225 gr. Speer, IMR-4350 63.0 gr. 2562 fps

Author with his 338 Hawk on Kodiak Island.

Graydon Snapp working up one grain at a time, found the 358 Hawk cartridge could deliver significantly more punch than the 35 Whelen. Here are four of his loads:

200gr. Hornady, AAC-2700 65.0gr. 2857 feet per second (fps)

250gr. Hawk, Varget 60.0gr. 2565 fps

250gr. Hornady, Varget 62.0gr. 2707 fps

250gr. Hornady, H-4895 61.0gr. 2728 fps

Below is a target shot by Ken Kempa, gun writer, while he was testing the 358 Hawk with pistol bullets. The accuracy was a little surprising since the twist on his barrel was really better suited to rifle weight bullets.

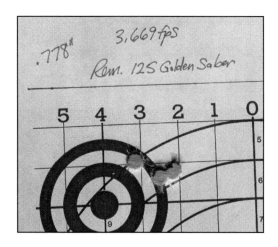

The 338 Hawk delivers very nearly everything that the 338 Winchester Magnum does. The 358 Hawk is virtually a twin for the 358 Norma Magnum. Recoil is much lower than these magnums. Hawk cartridges use less powder than do the magnum cases mentioned.

About the time the 338 and 358 Hawk were finished up, Bob called Graydon with an idea; he necked one of his 375 Hawk cases up to accept a .411 bullet. Fred and Graydon played with .411 and .416 bullets in the Hawk cases for a while. It quickly became apparent that the 411 Hawk was the way to go, the 416 reduced the shoulder area enough that it would have been nearly impossible to form and load the brass safely.

Before the end of 1996 Fred asked Bob Fulton to name this line of cartridges. Bob had designed and developed the Hawk line of bullets and at that time still owned Hawk Laboratories. He named the line... you guessed it, "HAWK." By the time a name was selected, Fred had come up with designs for everything from 240 Hawk to 3200 Hawk in addition to the larger cartridges.

Performance wise, Hawk Cartridges deliver magnum results with out the belt, and with less recoil.

We now had four exciting and useful cartridges (338, 358, 375, and the 411 Hawk). They have no belt, and still offer magnum power. They are accurate and yet reliable feeding cartridges. Brass is cheap and easy to locate. They are easy to form even for a novice, well maybe the 411 needs a more experienced hand.

Photo by www.mountainsunphotoart.com

The headspace myth, that just won't die.

We have all heard the old saw about small shoulders being insufficient to headspace on. More than likely the headspace myth came about as a result of the 400 Whelen, most versions used a standard 06 case and the shoulder was non-existent, to be kind.

The original 400 Whelen had a .458" shoulder, and later cartridges which have enough shoulder have suffered at the hands of this old myth. The problem is, over the years writers have repeated the myth without looking to the source, or checking for themselves. Michael Petrov investigated the 400 Whelen and proved that the writers all had it wrong. You can read that story in full in the chapter titled, "Smashing the Headspace Myth."

Petrov's research for the Whelen applies directly to the 411 Hawk as well. The shoulder has been proven sufficient for headspace over and over again. This in the hands of responsible reloaders who understand the importance of headspace. At the same time cartridges like the 400 Whelen and the 411 Hawk would not be good commercial offerings because the headspace is more critical than with most cartridges.

At Left: Graydon Snapp's daughter Anna, he says she will not give his 375 Hawk back.

We have tested 411 Hawk brass to see if it is possible to move the shoulder. Frankly, because of the Hawk's expanded shoulder diameter, it takes a great deal of concentrated effort to move the shoulder of the case once fully formed. You will not move the shoulder accidentally. Or to put it another way, it takes three men and a small boy working together to change it.

Wayne van Zwoll stopped in at the shop to talk about Hawk cartridges in 1997. He was reluctant as most experienced shooters are when somebody makes claims for their new wildcat. He seemed concerned about the shoulder and headspace. We set him up with a chambered barrel some fully formed brass and asked him to see what it would take to change the headspace. When he was done testing he ordered a 411 Hawk for his personal collection. That says 'everything' about the headspace issue.

Perhaps the best acid test for a cartridge is to put it in the hands of several shooters. Fred has shipped more 411 Hawks than any other cartridge in the line. The results are interesting, clients report that fire forming the brass requires a little more attention to detail, but *nobody who followed the forming instructions has had trouble with the shoulder.*

Over the years Hawk Cartridges have been written up in numerous articles and eventually found their way into "Cartridges of the World". A few additions have been made since those early days. One client asked for a 348 Hawk, bullet selection is limited, but to each his own. Then a 9.3mm Hawk, this amounts to an improved 9.3x62. Today you can order correctly head stamped brass for nearly all of the Hawk

Cartridges from Quality Cartridge, P.O. Box 445, Hollywood, MD 20636. They can be found on the web at: http://www.qual-cart.com

The newest addition to the line is the 19 Hawk. It uses the 7.62x39 Russian case so brass is cheap and readily available, one of the Hawk cartridge requirements. Data is included here for this newcomer; accuracy is awesome with groups in the teens during our tests. The birth of the 19 Hawk is tied to the book Fred Zeglin wrote on "Wildcat Cartridges" in 2005.

At Right: *19 Hawk and a 38 Special*

Next a 20 Hawk will come along. You can bet that ballistics will be pretty similar to the 19 Hawk, but the first question that came up when the 19 was being tested was, "Why not a 20?" Fred's answer was "Because I wanted a 19."

It's like the old joke about the cowboy in the cat house; his "date" pointing at his equipment and laughing asked, "Who you gonna please with that?" To which the cowboy replied with a smile and his thumb in his chest, "ME!"

You can't please everyone.

30-06 Springfield

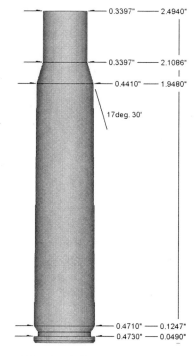

0.3397" ——— 2.4940"

0.3397" ——— 2.1086"

0.4410" —— 1.9480"

17deg. 30'

0.4710" —— 0.1247"
0.4730" —— 0.0490"

[Case Cap. 68.20 gr.]

Hunt of the Crimson Caterpillars.

The flight into Kodiak is an experience every traveler should have, not many landings include sharp turns and short runways. We flew out of Anchorage on ERA Airlines. On the flight over I noticed a guy sitting across the isle and a couple of rows ahead. He was wearing some boots that were well worn and I thought to my self, "Now there are a set of boots that have seen some miles!"

After we landed we went into the airport and collected our bags and when Mike Horstman, owner of Kodiak Guide Service was not waiting for us I figured he would be along soon. Then the guy with the well-worn boots walked up and asked if I was Fred Zeglin, and introduced himself as Ben Stevenson. I had been long-distance friends with his parents for years. Ed (Ben's Dad) had me build him a couple of custom 1895 Browning lever guns in 411 Hawk, but that's another story.

Ben Stevenson

Ben said that Mike had asked him to be our guide for this trip, that was just fine by me, Ben is the son of Ed and Deb Stevenson, owners of Sheep River Outfitters. Ed Stevenson grew up on a ranch in Wyoming where skills with horses, trapping, and guiding big game hunters were developed. Ed is a licensed Master Guide and outfitter, with over 45 years experience, his sons grew up working with Ed in Sheep River Hunting camps.

The week before we arrived there had been 3.5 feet of snow and the deer had been forced down from the high country, my email from Mike 4 days before we left on the hunt was simple, "3.5 feet of snow deer can't get off the beach, pick you up on the 16th."

Ben told us that he had talked to Mike on the phone just before the flight out of Anchorage and that he would be along to pick us all up in just a few minutes.

We ran into a hunter in the Airport that was waiting for the flight out, it turned out he was in camp with Mike the week before. He said it was the most fun he had ever had, he and seen lots of bucks. Then he assured us that even though the snow was mostly gone that we should have good hunting. I wondered, because even I know blacktail deer would prefer to be in the high country if the snow does not force them down. When Mike arrived there was a round of introductions and we loaded up to head for camp.

The first day is normally spent getting to camp. Mike informed us that they had already made a supply run and that we just had to load our gear in the boat and head out. From the boat launch it's about a twenty-minute ride to the camp. I enjoy this part of the trip as much as any other, there are always things to see along the way as we float past several small islands and peninsulas that jut out from Kodiak Island itself.

Mike Horstman in a comfortable glassing spot.

Kodiak Guide Service has a permanent camp with a cabin on Sharatin Bay. It's a rustic but comfortable, and most importantly a DRY place to stay. The main floor is the living room, kitchen, and dining room all in one with a sleeping loft above. Upon arriving in camp we were introduced to Nate Evans, he was a young guy whom Mike had agreed to train that season.

Kodiak can be pretty wet in November, so having a warm dry place to come back to is pretty desirable. We pack fairly light but all our hunting gear is water-proof and we make sure there are a couple of changes so that things can dry out before we have to wear them again. Wool as it is on most cold weather hunts is a great choice, but with the short days and long cold damp nights it should be mandatory dress for Alaska.

Mike guides for Kodiak Bears, Black Tailed Deer, Mountain Goat, Caribou, Moose, Black Bear, and Sheep. Obviously he hunts in areas other than just Kodiak. He has a long list of happy clients and can provide references. He tells me that he can make the hunt fit the clients needs and desires. For instance, some guys prefer to camp out or operate from spike camps, such services are available. Women are welcome in camp and many clients bring wives or daughters, while some hunt, some just come along for the experience.

In the morning, the smell of sausage cooking wafted up from the main floor. The occasional flicker of a flashlight in the predawn darkness of the cabin loft marked the beginning of the first day of our hunt on Kodiak. After a hearty breakfast of fried potatoes, eggs, and sausage we piled onto the boat and headed across the bay from our cabin.

Mike and Ben discussed the plans for the days hunt while we motored across the bay. It was decided that we would hunt up a long valley and depending on how things turned out we would either back track to the beach or head to an alternate pick up spot to the southeast of where we landed.

Mike pointed the boat toward the peninsula where we planned to spend the day. Mike is just the kind of guy I like to hunt with, he has a great sense of humor he is also an experienced and tough Master Guide. When I hunted deer with Mike a couple of years earlier, we came off the hill with my first blacktail buck, Mike told our camp mate for that trip, Bill Hughes that I had passed the hiking and shooting test. I was too tired to respond.

Deer were fairly scarce that first trip and the head from the one buck that I had manage to bag was swiped from it's hanging place by a fox when we went to town one afternoon. Mike felt bad about that and wanted me to come back so I could take home more than just some great pictures. In fact, he expressly asked me to bring my teen-aged son, along on the next trip, that's how this second hunt came to be.

Not long after I got home Mike sent me two fox pelts. The foxes came up to the cabin while we were playing cards in the evening. A pretty nice gesture and I like to think that one of them got his just deserts for stealing my bucks head.

Upon landing we put on packs, filled magazines and Ben struck out in the lead. Dewain, my son 15 years old at the time followed, I was next, and finally Nate our packer brought up the rear.

Nate proved right away that he could spot deer, he was the first to point out a doe on the rim ahead of us. We hunted uphill (I contend there is no downhill on Kodiak) slowly glassing as we went, at each bench along the ridge we stopped to glass the surrounding area.

Devil's Club

For those of you who have not hunted Kodiak, there is a weed that grows on the island called "Devil's club". The truly amazing thing about this weed is that it only grows in places where a hunter would need a hand-hold, at least that's how it seemed to me. Dewain claimed that it only grew in places where he fell down.

The sun is slow to rise this far north but it was obvious that this was going to be a clear day with blue skies and broad vistas. On my previous trip we had only one nice clear day so I new this was the day to get the camera out.

By mid-morning we were well above the beach and even though we had seen numerous doe by then I had

a thought that most flatlanders would have...
"that was a lot of hiking with no promise of results."

Ben Stevenson, glassing for Blacktail Deer from a bench top.

We continued to glass and see doe bedded along the ridgelines, from these vantage points the deer could see both directions off their ridge. They would look at us and keep track of our location. Ben said, " So long as they can see us they won't take off, but if we move out of sight they will get nervous and head for the next hill."   He was right, they never seemed to be concerned about us so long as we were visible.

The rut was getting underway so wherever we saw doe we spent time looking for bucks nearby. About the time I figured we had gone about as far from the beach as we could go and still make it down in daylight Nate and Ben spotted 3 bucks on a ridge above us. Ben, took us down the back side of our ridge so the bucks could not see us approach. We worked our way up a draw and up the next ridge, Ben glassed over the top and shook his head, no deer in sight. So, we moved over the top and headed higher in an effort to move above the position where the bucks were last seen.

We neared the crest of a ridge, dropped our packs under a tree and Ben crooked a finger at Dewain to follow him.

They quietly moved up the ridge to a lone spruce tree, and crawled under the bows at the base so I knew the buck was not far beyond. Some time passed before we heard one shot, then I heard Ben say to Dewain, "He's down, hit him again for insurance." After the second shot Ben slapped Dewain on the back and proclaimed, "Good Job." Just moments later they crawled back out from under the spruce tree, looked back at us, and we were off to take some pictures with Dewain's first blacktail buck.

Many years earlier I had built an ultra light weight 308 Winchester for my Dad on a small ring 98 Mauser, when Dewain turned fourteen his Grandpa passed that gun along to his name sake. He was carrying that gun on this hunt, after shooting his buck he had a pretty good cut on his eyebrow where the scope had popped him. I laughed at him and took pictures like any loving father would.

As soon as we had the pictures out of the way, Ben excused himself and slipped over the ridge. While we were still finishing up the congratulations and picture taking Ben returned and said to me, "Come on, there's another buck over here for you."

So we slipped over the ridge through the next swale and worked under another spruce tree much like the one my son had crawled under just a few moments earlier. Ben pointed to a buck on the next ridge, still lying in his bed, watching us. He check with the range finder, 128 yards, so there would be no need for hold over or adjustments of any kind just point and shoot.

Ben asked me to let him know when I was ready to shoot, I could see that he was ready to spot for me. I first took Ben's pack and slid it in front of me for a rest, then I pushed my day pack up on top of his empty pack. I was laying in a bowl shaped depression under the tree and needed to elevate my gun because the buck was slightly above us.

At the same time my feet were curled up high behind me, I was forced to arch my back to get a sight picture. In just a few seconds I was situated and ready to shoot. I was still breathing hard after climbing from where Dewain and our packer Nate were busy dressing out his buck. I looked thru the scope and at first I saw the not so desirable transition; from dirt... to deer... to sky, then my view cycled up and down thru that same batch of choices. I told Ben I had to catch my breath, he said, "We have all day, so long as he knows where we are he won't move."

A successful Hunt.

Concentrating on my breathing it didn't take long to get it under what I thought was control. I told Ben I was ready, There was a small mound of dirt and grass right were the heart and lungs were. The head, neck, part of the front shoulder, and the spine were clearly visible. I did not want to shoot the buck in the neck, he had a beautiful double white patch on his neck, I could already imagine what a great looking mount he would make (a common mistake). So I decided I would aim for the shoulder near where it met the mound of dirt, thinking this would be a kill shot, and I was certain it would anchor him.

The first shot completely missed, I don't have an excuse, the gun shoots ¾ minute of angle average, so it had to be me. Ben said with some urgency in his voice, "You missed." By now the buck was on his feet, which of course made available a larger kill zone. I quickly cycled the bolt aimed just behind the front shoulder and fired again. Ben reported, "Good shot, he's dead."

Something warm ran down the side of my nose. I reached up and discovered that I had duplicated my son's feat of collecting a Crimson Caterpillar only moments after he had. I said, "I will never live this down." Ben said, "What?" I turned toward him and he laughed.

At the shot the buck had lurched forward and quickly dropped out of sight. Ben backed out from our hiding spot and started toward the last place we had seen my buck. I followed as fast as a flatlander can.

I cleared the top of the ridge, Ben was standing just over the top and about 20 feet to my right. There was blood on the snow in the direction the buck had headed. The trail headed straight down toward some thick brush in the bottom of the next draw. I said, "Oh great, right to the bottom I suppose." Then I looked over at Ben he was grinning, in a flat tone he said, "Well, I guess we'll have to find him."

He traced the blood trail with a sweep of his arm and pointed to his right. Just passed where Ben was standing, maybe another 20 feet or so lay my buck, where he had circled. Then I saw the amusement on his face as Ben said, "Oh, there he is." with mock surprise in his voice. We both laughed and the inspection and photo session ensued.

Ben dressed him out cut him in half and it was not long before he was in Ben's pack and we were headed back to see if Dewain and Nate were ready to head for the boat. It's amazing to me how much shorter the hike is when you headed toward the beach and you have a deer in the bag.

Father and Son with matching scope cuts.

We met up with Mike in the boat and headed back to camp. There was a lot of laughter and joking about the fact that we managed to bag two deer and two caterpillars in the same day.

In truth, we had the best Father/Son hunt that I could have asked for. Dewain had a second deer tag to fill on that hunt, but nothing compares to the first! Take your kids hunting, you will never regret it.

Left to Right, Mike Horstman, Dewain Zeglin, Fred Zeglin, and Nate Evans.

Spot the deer. It's no easier in color.

Horstman's Kodiak Guide Service

P.O. Box 8286

Kodiak, AK 99615

907-942-7738

Web Site: www.kodiakguideservice.com

Alaska Frontier Guides

Ben Stevenson

P.O. Box 1222

Chickaloon, AK 99674.

(907) 232-4620

Web Site: http://www.alaskafrontierguides.com

Right to Left, 338 Hawk, 358 Hawk, 375 Hawk/S, and 411 Hawk.
These are the cartridges that started this successful line-up.

Super Six

For effective hunting rifles, don't rule out the 6mm

Deer and Big Game Rifles 2003
Reprinted here by permission http://www.tactical-life.com

Photos by www.mountainsunphotoart.com

Wayne Van Zwoll

You don't hear much about 6mm cartridges these days. More-powerful rounds get most of the press, and magnum cases don't mate easily with .243 bullets. Necking a .300 Remington Ultra Mag or a .30-378 Weatherby to .243 has little to recommend it. Even the short magnums have more capacity than can be used efficiently behind a 6mm bullet. As for standard hulls, we've already "sixed" almost all of them. The .243 Winchester is an altered .308 Winchester, and the 6mm Remington a necked-down 7x57 Mauser. You'll find few 6mm-06s on used-gun racks, but Weatherby's .240 has essentially the same case volume. Wildcatters have put the 6mm-.250 Savage on the charts as the 6mm Donaldson (30-degree shoulder) and the 6mm International (with the shoulder pushed back to reduce case capacity).

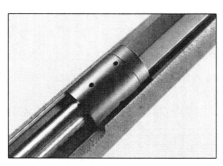

My field experience with the various sixes is pretty limited. Long ago I owned a 722 Remington in .244 Remington, a cartridge that appeared in 1955. The 722 had a 1-in-12 twist that stabilized bullets as heavy as 85 grains but was reported marginal with 100-grain spitzers. Winchester's .243, which came along the same year, was chambered in barrels bored 1-in-10. Most hunters who bought 6mms, it seemed, wanted to shoot deer, not just 'chucks and prairie dogs. Partly because the press claimed inadequate twist for heavy bullets in .244s and partly because Model 70s were available in .243, the Winchester round became more popular.

In 1963, with the advent of its Model 700, Remington adopted a 1-in-10 twist in 6mm barrels and renamed the .244. As the 6mm Remington, it has fared better at market. If lion's round has a fault, it's in the parent case. The 7x57 is a centenarian cartridge that's hard not to like—in Mauser rifles. You see, Paul Mauser designed his famous 1898 action around the 57mm hull. It's longer than the 51mm case of the .308 Winchester, shorter than the .30-06 Springfield. To fit cartridges with 57mm brass into an action built around the .308, you have to seat bullets deep, reducing usable case volume and velocity. Short actions commonly used in 6mm and .243 rifles give no advantage to the longer 6mm Remington case. In long actions, the 6mm can be hand loaded to significantly higher speeds. But with a long action, why not chamber a .25-06 Remington?

Or, if you must have a 6mm, why not try the .240 Hawk?

The Hawk line was developed by Fred Zeglin (www.z-hat.com) of Casper. It's based on the .30-06 case, with the shoulder blown forward and given a 25-degree slant. When I first met Zeglin years ago, the unassuming young man had built only a couple of rifles with Hawk chambers. One was a .358 for hunting partner Graydon Snapp. Snapp praised his .358 Hawk, claiming almost as much horsepower as the .358 Norma Magnum with 200-grain bullets at 2,800 fps.

A 6mm wasn't on Zeglin's agenda then. The big case was better suited to huskier bullets. He built a .411 for me on a commercial Mauser action, fitting it with a Douglas barrel, a stick of curly maple and Ashley iron sights. Full-power loads with 300-grain bullets reached 2,500 fps, matching the .375 H&H and exceeding the punch of many traditional "elephant" cartridges.

Zeglin eventually necked the Hawk case to .243. "What would you need that for?" I asked. A .240 on a bigger case than the standard '06 seemed about as useful as a rocket-powered Yugo. "Overbore" by any definition, the .240's ratio of case to bore volume all but equals that of the .244 Belted Rimless Holland & Holland Magnum, a necked-down .300 H&H introduced in 1955.

Zeglin grinned. "What color do you want the stock?"

Zeglin built the rifle on a Model 700 Remington action, installing a 28-inch Douglas octagon barrel heavy enough to anchor a yacht. The H-S Precision stock, painted red on special order, had clean lines and a good feel. A Weaver 6-20x40 Grand Slam scope in Talley rings completed the outfit.

My first two shots from the 240 Hawk slipped into one hole. Subsequent rounds clustered close by. Only bullets heavier than 85 grains failed to shoot inside 3/4 inch. That was predictable. Zeglin and I had agreed that this would be a varmint rifle. The 1-in-14 rifling twist was tailored to lightweight bullets.

I was especially impressed with the .240's metal finish, a satin blue by Phil Filing (307-436-2330, www.gunbluing.com), who has lived in Glenrock for about a decade. "It's a Teflon treatment," Filing told me, 'a baked-on finish That's really more durable than blue." It costs just a little more and is offered in five colors. Also, it bonds to any metal alloy. "The surface must have some texture," Filing said. "We bead-blasted this rifle with aluminum oxide; it's as fine as baking soda. Some companies use coarse glass beads that make the surface rougher than I prefer." Filing finishes all Talley mounts. "Talley's shop is next door," he said, smiling. "We don't waste money shipping."

The 240 Hawk holds a little more powder than the flat-shooting 240 Weatherby, which kicks 90-grain bullets downrange at 3,500 fps. Zeglin anticipated 4000 fps with 60-grain bullets. "Maybe you can do even better," he said as we tossed the rifle in my Suzuki. It sounded like a challenge.

I started conservatively, my first loads nudging bullets along at idle. The first hint of trouble came with an 80-grain bullet clocking 3,591 fps ahead of 54 grains of Winchester 760. The bolt opened easily enough, but the primer was gone. I fired again and got a cracked case. Excess headspace, I thought. So it proved to be. I found the problem in the die setting. The custom dies were a bit too short for a "kiss fit" at the top of the ram stroke. In other words, full-length resizing reduced head-to-shoulder measure to below spec. So when the striker hit the primer, it drove the too-short case deeper into the chamber. Expanding gas inside the case ironed the pliable front of the case to the chamber walls while kicking back against the primer and head. Separations and lost primers resulted. Adjusting the die was easy. I just place a fired case onto the ram at the top of its stroke and turned down the die until it contacted the case. Then I lowered the ram and gave the die an eighth of a turn down. I ran the case up again and checked the fit in the chamber, repeating the routine until the bolt closed easily but snugly on the case.

Groups with lightweight bullets at high speed stayed around 3/4 inch. And there's not much need for a 100-grain bullet in a 6mm.

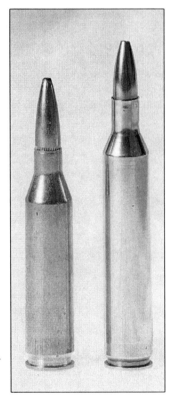

Some hunters will disagree. But 85-grain bullets driven into the forward ribs of deer-size animals kill like lightning. The blistering speed of the .240 Hawk can make long shots easier, partly because you'll use less holdover, more importantly because they'll be less affected by wind—which, unlike gravity, varies in its effect.

Sure, this Hawk is inefficient. So is an F-16. Sometimes performance matters most. Fred Zeglin keeps busy these days building takedown rifles—from Model 95 lever-action Winchesters to Model 70s. But I'll long remember that first 4,000-fps reading from an 80-grain bullet....

I had no more problems with cases. On the next page are a few cream-puff loads for the .240 Hawk.

Above: *243 Winchester vs. 240 Hawk*

.240 Hawk First Round of testing.

Charge (grs.), powder	Bullet weight (grs.), Brand	Velocity (fps)
52, H4350	60, Sierra	3,550
55, H4831	85, Sierra	3,325
58, 3100	89, Gardiner	3,537 (accurate!)
54, Big Game	90, Remington	3,474
54, N160	90, Remington	3,223
58, RL-22	100, Nosler Partition	3,420
58. H4831	100, Nosler Partition	3,480
58, WMR	105, Speer	3,358
58, RL-25	105, Speer	3,260

.240 Hawk Second Round of testing.

My second round of loads for the .240 Hawk was more ambitious, because I knew what to expect of the powders. Even with throat-burning acceleration, the long, heavy barrel kept recoil and muzzle jump down. Here's a short list of loads that delivered super performance. Approach them with caution!

Charge (grs.), powder	Bullet weight (grs.), type	Velocity (fps)
51, Win 748	75, Hornady	3,954
50. Varget	75, Hornady	3,990 (1/2")

Continued on next page…

Charge (grs.), powder	Bullet weight (grs.), type	Velocity (fps)
52, 4895	80, Remington	4,037 (1/2")
53, RL-15	80, Remington	4,055
58, 4350	85, Sierra	4,040 (3/4", maximum)
56, Win 760	85, Sierra	4,010 *(1/2" maximum)*
57, Big Game	85, Sierra	4,138 (excessive!)
56, H380	88, Berger	3,910 (maximum)
58, RL-19	88, Berger	3,927
58, H4831SC	90, Speer	3,804 (1-1/4")
55, N150	90, Speer	4,014 (excessive!)
60, RL-22	90, Speer	3,931
59, WMR	100, Hornady	3,867
59, M3100	100, Sierra	3,935 (excessive!)
59, Big Boy	105, Speer	3,662

MEET THE GUNSMITH
Z-Hat Custom

Reprinted here by permission of Guns Magazine and Publishers Development Corporation. This article first appeared on the May, 2004 issue of Guns Magazine.

Photo by www.mountainsunphotoart.com

Dick Williams

For those of you who have not been to Wyoming, there are a number of reasons that firearms enthusiasts love the state. First, it is spectacularly beautiful. Second, it is a hunting Mecca with a large and diverse population of game animals. Third, it's shooter friendly. Finally, it's very sparsely populated, with major cities being about the size of residential suburbs located outside major metropolitan areas elsewhere in the United States. This means that if you're in the gun business, you can't expect a large walk in crowd. So any gunsmith living in Wyoming had better be good enough to attract an out of state clientele. Fred Zeglin is more than a good gunsmith.

Fred has a company called Z-Hat Custom located in Casper, Wyoming, and he does build custom rifles. He also has a series of custom cartridges and makes custom loading dies for shooters ordering a rifle chambered in one of these calibers. His work in all three of these areas is outstanding. But as usual when I get excited, I get ahead of myself.

Paying His Dues

Fred cut his teeth in the gun business working for an established gun shop in Coeur d'Alene, Idaho right after graduating from Lassen College with his degree in gunsmithing. Rifles were king in Idaho. By the time he left several years later, Fred was shop foreman scheduling the work of several other gunsmiths while still doing projects himself.

Moving to San Diego, California, Fred became the full time gunsmith for two large gun stores. In this Mediterranean climate, his work leaned more toward handguns and general repair. After four years in California and more than ten years experience in the business, Fred moved back to Wyoming where he had spent his boyhood. For the first two years back home, he operated a retail gun shop of his own. In 1996, he began marketing his multiple talents on the internet, and he hasn't looked back.

I didn't personally discover Fred. I received a phone call from Phil Filing at Glenrock Blue who had restored (more like rebuilt,) a Model 1897 Winchester trap gun for me (see GUNS, November 2001) Phil simply said there was a custom rifle builder in Casper who was pretty good and might interest me. If Phil thought he was "pretty good," I had to follow up.

A few minutes looking over the Z-Hat web site www.z-hat.com gave me some familiarity with the series of Hawk cartridges. Magnum velocities using plentiful, inexpensive, non-belted brass sounded like a good idea, and brought back youthful flights of fancy through the old P.O. Ackley loading manual. Perhaps this was my chance to shoot a truly custom rifle with enhanced performance and minimal abuse from recoil. A brief phone conversation with Fred confirmed his interest in doing a project. We settled quickly on the 264 Hawk cartridge because I had never worked with a 6.5mm rifle and because it is an extremely pleasant big game caliber to shoot. Deciding on the rifle took longer.

Building From Scratch

Fred will either build you a rifle from scratch or start with whatever you provide. You can send an action, a barreled action, or a complete rifle for him to work or rework. To show the full range of his talents, we decided on a rifle from scratch. He suggested a Mauser action with controlled round feeding, specifically a Charles Daly 98, and an XX premium Douglas barrel.

I'm not one of the "controlled feed" fanatics. In my many years of shooting Sakos and Remington 700s, I've never had a failure that wasn't caused by me screwing up the bolt stroke. And since the .264 caliber is not your charging buffalo stopper, the dangerous game argument didn't enter into the discussions.

I went with a controlled round feed system for the same reason I chose the caliber; I didn't have one. But it was when Fred mentioned he could install a Manlicher stock that my knees buckled. I am totally goofy about Manlichers!

The only downside is that most Manlichers feature barrels 20 inches or shorter, and I didn't want to give up velocity in an "improved" cartridge. When Fred said he could full stock a 22 inch barrel, I totally surrendered to his judgment. I can tell you unequivocally that I have not regretted that decision for one moment. Opening the box upon the rifle's arrival at my house was one of the most thrilling long gun moments of my life. I was looking at a thing of beauty designed specifically for me.

The stock is a triple A fancy Claro Walnut from Acra-Bond, has a low gloss finish, and is beautifully fitted to the barreled action. It had been equipped with front and rear sling swivels. Barrel and action have a Double Guard  finish, which is actually two finishes for extra protection from rust or corrosion of any kind. It's a matte blue with a coat of Teflon/Moly. The front end of the stock has the classic nose cap fitted, and it's finished in the same low gloss blue "Double Guard" as the barrel and action. A NECG 98 gas shield with a three-position safety has replaced the stock Mauser shield.

Special attention was paid to the iron sights. There is a fiber optic front sight covered by a hood with windows, both of which set on a Universal ramp with .030" elevation built in. The rear sight is a Classic Adjustable with a see through fiber optic insert. Fred also sent Talley's TNT rings and bases for a scope. These allowed the mounting of a Burris 3X-9X Fullfield II rifle scope while leaving the iron sights in place in case some kind of disaster in the field makes them necessary.

The rifle had also been equipped with a Universal Quick Lock Recoil Pad from NECG that can be slipped on and off over a base plate in the butt of the stock. If the rifle stock doesn't fit you, you simply slide on a pad of different thickness. It's an interesting feature and one well suited to a custom rifle. It wasn't until I started shooting that I realized how nice a job Fred did on the trigger; it has absolutely no creep and a consistent let off of 3¾ pounds.

Custom Cartridges

One drawback to most custom calibers is that you can't buy factory ammunition. Not so with the Hawk family. Z-Hat stocks loaded ammunition for several of their calibers including the 264 Hawk. In fact, Fred will develop loads for your rifle with any bullet weight you choose. This service will add to your bill because it does require range time. If you want to load your own ammo, data is not a problem since there is a CD loading manual available that can be provided with your rifle.

Fred tested my rifle with one load and sent data for several other suggested loads. He also provided a set of his full-length reloading dies for the .264 Hawk that includes an in-line seating die. This features a sliding sleeve inside the seating die body and an opening in the side of the die near the top. When you drop the bullet into the hole on the side of the die, it is caught by the sliding sleeve and held in position as you raise the shell case up into the seating die.

No need to hold the bullet on top of the case mouth with one hand while you raise the case with the other hand. This worked quite well with any bullet featuring at least a minimal boat tail, but required some finesse and fidgeting with the loading lever when flat base bullets were being loaded. I suspect that a little more case mouth chamfering would make things easier.

I originally thought this would be a "one load rifle," but I was kidding myself. When I like a rifle this much, I'm going to spend more time with it than one load would allow. I had a large can of IMR 4831, and it was one of the powders recommended for the 120 grain Nosler. I also used it for the 129 grain Hornady spire point and 140 grain Sierra boat tails although other powders were recommended for these.

The Nosler and Hornady bullets were loaded in some brass provided by Fred that was head stamped 264 Hawk. (Did I mention that properly head-stamped brass is available from Z-Hat for all the Hawk calibers?) I also fire formed some 270 Win cases by shooting 140 grain Sierra SBT seconds I had purchased years ago before Sierra moved from California to

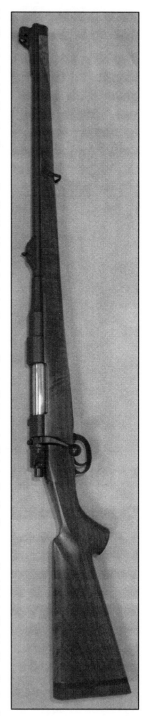

Missouri. The 270 cases formed perfectly looking like the Hawk cases after one firing.

Perhaps I was just lucky with the Noslers, or perhaps this rifle will shoot all the Z-Hat recommended loads into less than 1½ inches. Whatever the case, I dropped the powder charges a couple of grains, and my first two loads with the Nosler's produced 100 yard groups of less than one inch and less than 1½ inches at velocities over 3100 fps. The IMR 4831 was not as successful with the Hornady and Sierra bullets giving groups out around two inches.

264 Hawk   6.5-06 Ackley Improved

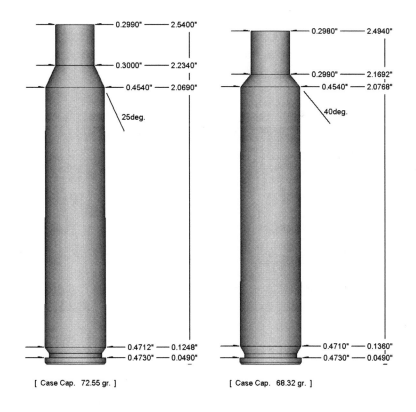

[Case Cap. 72.55 gr.]   [Case Cap. 68.32 gr.]

Certainly acceptable for hunting accuracy, (and I did take a young hog with the Sierra bullet,) but not up to Fred's standards of one inch or less for full stocked rifles (half stock sporters from Z-Hat will shoot under 1/2 inch at 100 yards FDZ).

I'm looking forward to some fun shooting sessions over the next year to see exactly how good this rifle is, and my suspicion is that staying with the recommended powders and primers will get me under one inch with any selected bullet.

Quality Has its Price

There's nothing cheap about Fred Zeglin's work, nor would you expect that to be the case. A truly custom rifle is very labor intensive, and every custom piece adds both material and fitting/finishing costs to the project. But before he cuts the first chip of metal or touches sandpaper to wood, Fred will walk you through the entire building process piece by piece. In the long run, it is your choice as to exactly what you want included in your custom rifle. I can't insure you he can do everything you want for the price you have in mind. What I do guarantee is that if you let him, he can fulfill your dream.

Selected Loads   .264 Hawk

Charge	Bullet	Velocity
57 grains IMR 4831	120 Nosler SBT	3139 fps
58 grains IMR 4831	120 Nosler SBT	3154 fps
55 grains IMR 4831	129 Hornady SP	2950 fps
52 grains IMR 4831	140 Sierra SBT	2749 fps

Thermodynamic Efficiency of the .300 Hawk Cartridge

Alvin Byars

Fred Zeglin, the gun guru at Z-Hat Custom has often made the comment that his Hawk line of cartridges were among "the most efficient cartridges available." Not ones to take boasting lightly, we at AEM Enterprises, Inc. decided to look closely at his claim. It turns out that Fred is right. And here's the proof.

The Laws of Thermodynamics

Before the math and science in this topic turn you off, please read on. Our intent is to lightly cover the immutable laws that govern how efficient any energy conversion can be. After all, that's what we're examining.

Classical Thermodynamics is the science that studies energy and the transformation of energy into work, or moving things around. When we speak of the thermodynamic efficiency of a cartridge, what we mean is the efficiency of the cartridge in transforming the chemical energy contained in the unfired propellant into the kinetic energy of the speeding bullet. Classical Thermodynamics is completely described by two laws.

The first law is often referred to as the conservation of mass and energy. Mass (or matter, the stuff of which things are made) and energy can be transformed from one into the other. But, the total amount of mass and energy after any transformation is the same as the total we started with before the transformation. Energy cannot be created or destroyed; it can only be changed from one form to another. They can only be changed from one form to another. This law also tells us that when we completely burn one pound of gunpowder, we are going to end up with one pound of gas. When we ignite the powder in a cartridge and release its energy, only part of the energy will be transformed into the bullet's motion. What doesn't get transformed into bullet motion is going somewhere, either barrel heat and wear, or hot gases, or unburned powder. But, none of it is just going to disappear. Another way of stating the first law of thermodynamics is "there's no such thing as a free lunch." This is common sense stuff.

The second law is even more common sense. It says that energy will always flow from high-energy sources to low energy sources. We are never going to get warm by hugging something colder than we are. Gunpowder is high-energy stuff. By comparison, a bullet moving down a barrel is low energy. When we ignite the gunpowder, the bullet is going to move. It's not going the other way. The second law also sets a limit on the transformation of energy. When we set something hot right up next to something cold, heat is going to flow from the hot thing to the cold thing until both things are the same temperature. Then the heat stops flowing between the two things.

The "model" most often used by thermodynamics to describe the transformation of heat energy into energy of motion is a piston in a cylinder being pushed by hot expanding gases. In this model, heat is injected into the cylinder, the pressure of the gas increases, the rising pressure moves the piston and increases the volume of the cylinder. As the volume of the cylinder increases, the pressure decreases and the temperature drops. Thermodynamics represents this model mathematically with the following equation:

$$P * V = n * R * T$$ where P is the pressure of the gas,

V is the volume of the gas,

n is the quantity of gas,

R is a number called the Universal Gas Constant, (about 1.25 for smokeless propellants), and T is the temperature of the gas.

Thermodynamics calls this the Equation of State. This model described by the Equation of State is completely analogous to the pressure of hot gases from ignited gunpowder pushing a bullet down the barrel of a gun.

You can relax now, because the above equation is the last one you are going to see in this article. Everything presented in the rest of this article can be derived from this equation. The important things to remember are these: The first law tells us that when we burn a pound of powder, we are going to get a pound of gas. The Equation of State tells us that as the temperature rises and more gas is produced, the pressure rises and pushes the bullet down the barrel. As the bullet moves down the barrel, the volume of gas behind the bullet increases, and the pressure and temperature drop. Finally, the second law tells us that chemical energy in the gun powder will continue to be transformed into increased bullet velocity until the gas pressure, volume and temperature reach some kind of equilibrium.

Thermodynamics and Cartridge Efficiency

One of the questions asked by thermodynamics is, "How much energy can I convert into work?" In our case, "What is the maximum velocity I can get from this cartridge?" Without going into a lot of mathematics, suffice it to say that it depends on only two things: the energy contained in the gunpowder, and the proportion of that energy that is converted into bullet motion. Common sense, isn't it?

The amount of chemical energy contained in a pound of pure gunpowder is pretty much the same from one gunpowder to the next, around 1,550,000 foot-pounds. The thing that changes from one gunpowder to the next is the burning rate. The shape of the powder and the coatings, deterrents and other additives determine the burning rate. These additives make up about 15% of the powder as it comes from the canister, so that the chemical energy contained in a pound of gunpowder out of the canister is about 1,325,000 foot-pounds. That is roughly 189 foot-pounds per grain of powder. For example, a cartridge that holds 75 grains of powder holds about 14,175 foot-pounds of chemical energy. If you take a look at Figure 1, you will see the chemical energy contained in five popular .308 caliber cartridges. This chart assumes that each cartridge has the bullet seated one caliber deep, that the case is completely filled with powder, and that the density of the powder is 0.85, which is typical for rifle powders. It is important to understand that when we speak of density here we are talking about the density of the powder itself, not the load density. In this case, the load density is 100%. The powder density (more correctly, the specific gravity or specific weight of the powder) is assumed to be 85%.

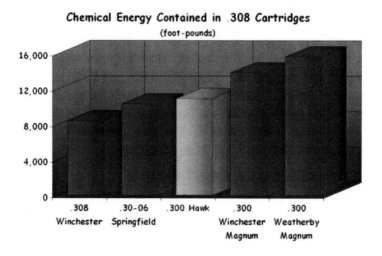

Chemical Energy Contained in .308 Cartridges
(foot-pounds)

Figure 1

The chart in Figure 1 is really nothing more than the case capacity of the five cartridges. However, rather than showing case capacity in terms of how many grains of water each case can hold, it is shown in terms of how many foot-pounds of chemical energy each case can hold when filled with gunpowder. Notice in the chart that the .300 Hawk is pretty average in its "energy capacity" as far as .308 caliber cartridges go, not much greater than the .30-06 Springfield.

Now, if all of these .308 caliber cartridges were equally efficient in converting chemical energy into projectile motion, then we would expect the .300 Hawk to be fairly average in terms of bullet velocity since it is fairly average in terms of energy capacity. However, take a look at Figure 2 on the next page.

Figure 2 shows the average velocity for the five .308 caliber cartridges with various bullet weights. These velocities are the average maximum velocities from several reloading manuals rounded off to the nearest 25 feet per second. As you can see, the velocities produced by the .300 Hawk are very close to those produced by the .300 Winchester Magnum, and right on the heels of the .300 Weatherby Magnum. Obviously, not all cartridges are equally efficient in converting chemical energy into bullet velocity.

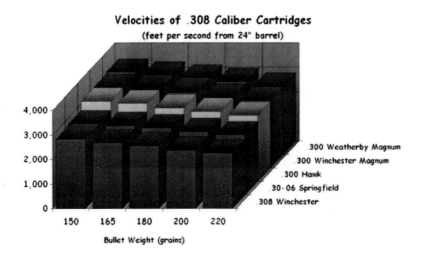

Velocities of .308 Caliber Cartridges
(feet per second from 24" barrel)

Bullet Weight (grains)

Figure 2

Perhaps even more interesting than the average velocities for the five .308 caliber cartridges are the kinetic energies. After all, that is what we are really interested in when we talk about cartridge efficiency. How efficient is the cartridge in converting the chemical energy in the gunpowder into kinetic energy of a speeding bullet?

Two interesting things can be seen in Figure 3. First, the average amount of kinetic energy produced by a given cartridge loaded to its maximum is pretty much the same regardless of bullet weight. Second, the kinetic energy produced by the .300 Hawk is very close to that produced by the .300 Winchester Magnum, and again right on the heels of the .300 Weatherby Magnum.

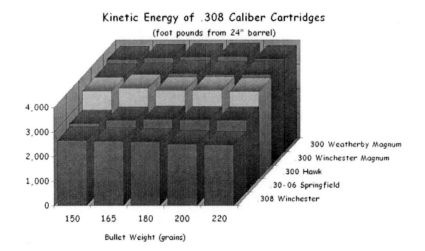

Figure 3

So, I can hear you asking, "What determines how efficient a cartridge is in converting chemical energy into bullet velocity?" Thermodynamics tells us that it is determined by three things:

1)   Volumetric expansion ratio

2)   Heat losses

3)   Pressure gradient in the barrel

The volumetric expansion ratio is nothing more that the total volume of the cartridge case plus the volume of the barrel, divided by the volume of the case.   Figure 4 shows the volumetric expansion ratios for our five .308 cartridges.

The expansion ratios shown in Figure 4 are based on 24 inch barrels.   The graph is sort of the opposite of the case capacities. In general, everything else being equal, smaller cartridges are more efficient and longer barrels are more efficient.   This is all based on the Equation of State.   But, the Equation of State describes an "ideal closed system" from which no energy can escape.   A cartridge igniting in a gun is a pretty open system and a heck of a lot of energy is lost to heat.

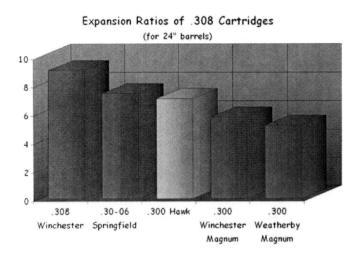

Figure 4

Below is shown the conversion of chemical energy that takes place in a typical rifle cartridge when the gunpowder is ignited:

Mechanical energy

Projectile motion   32%

Barrel friction   2%

Thermal energy

Hot gases   34%

Barrel heat   30%

Chemical energy

Unburned propellant   1%

As we can see, nearly two thirds of the chemical energy in the gunpowder goes to heat, either a hot barrel or hot gases. This is clearly illustrated in Figure 5.

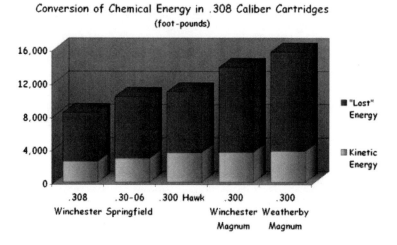

Conversion of Chemical Energy in .308 Caliber Cartridges
(foot-pounds)

Figure 5

The interesting thing to note in Figure 5 is that as we continue to increase cartridge size and chemical energy capacity in an attempt to get more velocity and kinetic energy, the decreasing expansion ratios quickly catch up with us and we reach a "point of diminishing returns." Beyond that point we produce a lot more heat, but not much more velocity and kinetic energy. Hence, heat loss is the second thing that determines cartridge efficiency.

The third thing that determines cartridge efficiency is the pressure gradient in the barrel. Figure 6 shows the estimated pressure gradient for the .300 Hawk with a 180-grain bullet leaving the muzzle at 3,000 feet per second, as graphically produced by the AccuLoad precision reloading program.

As can be seen in Figure 6 on the following page, pressure in the barrel quickly rises, reaching a maximum when the bullet has traveled a bit less than two inches, then gradually decreases until the bullet exits the barrel. The longer we can keep the pressure up in the barrel, the more chemical energy we will convert to kinetic energy and bullet velocity.

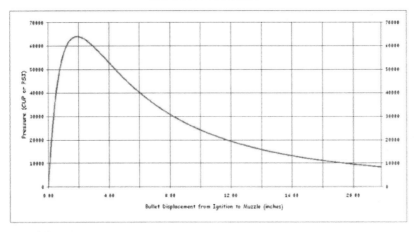

Estimated Barrel Pressure Gradient

Calculations based on LeDuc's Equation

Figure 6

Now, let's see if we can wrap all this up by taking a different view of the information shown in Figure 5. When we talk about the thermodynamic efficiency of a cartridge, we are really talking about the percentage of chemical energy contained in the cartridge's gunpowder that will be converted into kinetic energy of a speeding bullet. This is exactly what is shown in Figure 7.

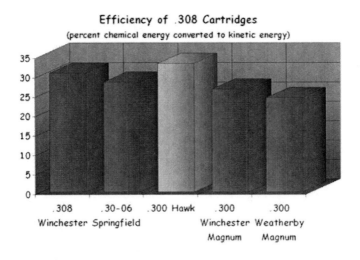

Efficiency of .308 Cartridges
(percent chemical energy converted to kinetic energy)

Figure 7

One thing is very clear from Figure 7. The .300 Hawk cartridge is considerably more efficient than other smaller or larger .308 caliber cartridges, based on the effective use of energy conversion.

Defining efficiency varies from one source to another; Pejsa defined it as a ratio of energy delivered at the muzzle as compared to the energy wasted in recoil. No mention was made in the examination of energy loss due to heat, etc. and the honors are always pointed toward the heaviest firearm. Another popular theory for efficiency is the ratio of velocity gained per grain of powder used. The major problem with this method is that the scale is tipped toward the smallest cartridge and bullet. In other words, the old .22 Rimfire Short will usually come out on top. As we have shown, efficiency can be based on the most effective use of the energy contained in the gunpowder. And in this light, the .300 Hawk really shines.

Smashing the Headspace Myth!

Editors Note: My apologies to those of you who read my "Wildcat Cartridges" book, as this article is repeating here. However, I feel that Mr. Petrov's research deserves to be widely shared as it dispels a myth that is oft repeated and seldom examined. Enjoy!

Excerpted from Precision Shooting, Magazine, Feb. 2001. Reprinted here by permission of Precision Shooting Magazine. Thanks to Michael Petrov for all his research, and willingness to share it with the shooting fraternity.

The .400 Whelen

MICHAEL PETROV

Major Townsend Whelen was instrumental in the development of a line of cartridges that were based on the 30 Government Model 1906 cartridge case. In this article I will try to trace the history and development of the Whelen-named cartridges until 1923. Much has been written about the Whelen-named cartridges as well as the many different adaptations of them in the last 80 years. I wish to return to the original source material as much as possible for the history on these cartridges. Much of the contemporary published material, especially on the .400, differs from what my research has turned up.

In the early 1920's Whelen tested some of the big bore British bolt guns and although he was impressed with the power of these rifles he was unhappy with their accuracy. He believed a rifle could be built in America with a more powerful cartridge than what was on the market following the First World War. At the same time he wanted to use the 1903 Springfield and the standard length Mauser action without going to the expense of using the larger and more expensive Magnum length actions. His first experimental work on these was before either of the two big gun companies had introduced a bolt action in .30-06 caliber (Remington M-30 1921 & Winchester M-54 1923). From 1923 to1925 Griffin & Howe only offered their proprietary Whelen cartridges as their largest caliber rifles and not any of the English cartridges such as the .375 H&H. A .375 H&H bolt action rifle From Holland & Holland would have set a sportsman back $400 In 1922.

.38 WHELEN: (.375 Whelen)

The first reference I can find that discusses the idea of necking up the .30-06 case is in a letter from Townsend Whelen to the gunmaker Fred Adolph of New York dated August 23, 1919. Whelen is trying to get a barrel for the .38 Whelen cartridge that he and Adolph 0. Niedner are working on. The .38 Whelen is the .30-06 necked-up to use the Winchester 275-grain .38-72 W.C.F. bullet re-formed with a spire point. In the January 1923 American Rifleman, Whelen is sending people to Niedner at Dowagiac, Michigan because Niedner is now making the .38 Whelen. By April 1st of 1923 Whelen announces that Winchester is stopping the production of the 275-grain .38-72 WCF bullets and suggests that no more .38 Whelens be made. I am not sure if any of these rifles survived the last eighty years but it's not because I have not looked for them. This cartridge was reintroduced in the 1950's and named the .375 Whelen. I have often wondered what the outcome of the .35 & .400 Whelen would have been if there had been a supply of good .375" bullets back in 1923.

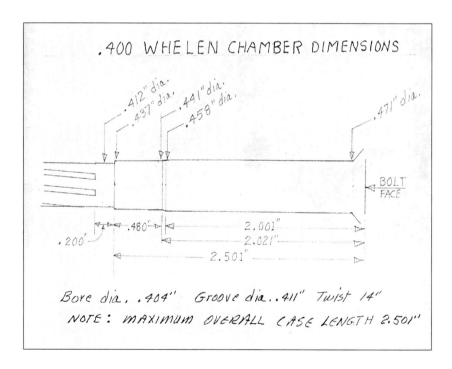

.400 WHELEN CHAMBER DIMENSIONS

Bore dia. .404" Groove dia. .411" Twist 14"
NOTE: MAXIMUM OVERALL CASE LENGTH 2.501"

WAR DEPARTMENT

OFFICE OF THE CHIEF OF STAFF

WASHINGTON

August 23, 1919

Fred Adolph, Esq.
    Genoa, New York.

Dear Mr. Adolph:

Your letter of the 18th instant relative to the barrels received. When you hear from Zischang please let me know. It is a pretty expensive job getting a new nickel steel barrel from the Winchester Company at the price they now ask ($20.), and then having it rebored for $18. However I now have on hand a .25 caliber Winchester single shot rifle, the barrel of which is getting pitted due to the smokeless primers in the small .25-20 shells. I may want, in the course of a month or so, to have this barrel rebored to .38 caliber with an 18 inch twist, groove diameter about .375, bore diameter about .365-inch. If I decide to do this, and Zischang can do the job, I will send it to him. I do not want this barrel chambered as Neidner will chamber it for me.

In addition to this I am anxious to get a heavy nickel or Krupp steel barrel, about 28 inches long, .38 caliber, bored exactly as above, for fitting to a Springfield action. Neidner and I have been trying to develop a .38 caliber high power Springfield for some time, to use the regular Springfield shell, obtaining the shells before they are necked down, and then necking them down to .38 caliber. This barrel will be chambered with the regular Mann-Neidner chamber, and will use the .38-275 Winchester soft point jacketed bullet slightly altered in form in a swedge. This will make a most excellent big game rifle. Now I imagine that we will have to go to Germany for such barrels, so as soon as you find out anything about getting barrels from Germany please let me know and I will take the matter up with you and let you know exactly what is wanted.

There is a market at present for reloading tools, particularly for tools for the .30-1906 cartridge, and for a press and resizing die which will resize .30-1906 shells once fired to standard size. This is just a suggestion.

Very sincerely,

[signature]

How the prices have gone up! Winchester are now charging $60 for a .22 Single Shot rifle that they used to sell for $15.

.400 WHELEN:

The first notice I find of the .400 Whelen is in "Arms And The Man" on June15, 1922 where Whelen tells about his work on this cartridge. The .400 Whelen is the 30-06 cylindrical case necked down to take the .405 Winchester 300gr. .411" diameter round nose bullet. Four test rifles were being made up, two on the 1903 Springfield and two on the Mauser action. Whelen estimates the velocity of the 300-gr. bullets at 2350-2600 fps. These test rifles, as well as the loading tools, were made by James V. Howe then of Philadelphia, Pennsylvania. The barrels for these were made and installed by A.O. Niedner in Dowagiac, Michigan. By November 15th, 1922 Whelen was offering a circular by mail with information on the 400. Anyone know where one of these circulars is to be found?

I can not think of another cartridge with as bad a reputation as the .400 Whelen. From Cartridges of the World 6th Edition "The .400 Whelen was not a very successful development because when the 30-06 case neck is expanded to this size it leaves only a very slight shoulder and this gives rise to serious headspace problems." I have also read several reports of the firing pin driving the case forward over the shoulder.

I am not going to list all the negative things I have read about the .400 or there would be room for little else. As I began to collect information there were two distinct schools of thought on the .400; One was by people who used the .400 and thought it was a fine cartridge; the other was by those who did not, telling you how bad it was. The first praise I read for the .400 was by, (and it should be no surprise to the readers), Elmer Keith. A quote from Big Game Rifles by Elmer Keith, Samworth 1935. "I have used this rifle over a period of eleven years and have a lot of respect for it." "Much criticism has been passed on this rifle and cartridge, some claiming that the front shoulder of the ease was sufficient to hold its headspace against the blow of the firing pin. Such is not the case, and that forward shoulder is ample in correctly chambered rifles and used with correctly necked cases."

The biggest challenge I faced in learning about the .400 was to find and record chamber dimensions of the older original rifles.

Although it was not a popular cartridge there have been several .400's made over the last 78 years. Most of the problems with this cartridge I have been able to trace to one factor. The. 30-06, .25 Whelen (.25-06), .35 Whelen and .38 Whelen all have a shoulder diameter of .441. "The ORIGINAL .400 Whelen shoulder is .458". When and how this information got lost to modern riflemen and writers I have no idea. Many 400's that were made in later years for which I have measurements have the .441" shoulder; this is also true of many resizing dies.

I have wanted a .400 Whelen rifle for some time and my search for an early. 400 Whelen has not been easy. The rifles I found either had been modified or the price was well out of my reach. Which brings up a good point. If these things are no good why are they so expensive? Sorry. Back to the story.

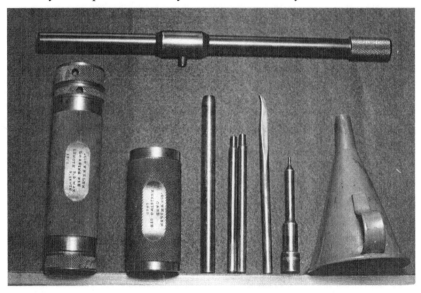

Figure 2 Whelen's personal loading tools for the .400 Whelen

By the time I had resigned myself to the fact that I might never find what I was looking for, a chain of events began that you only dream about as a collector. Not only was I able to acquire what I believe to be the second .400 Whelen Made by Griffin & Howe in their first year (1923), it showed up unfired with a box of G&H cartridges. These early G&H's had blued bolts and there was not so much as a brass rub mark on the bolt face. The icing on the cake was when friends Mark Benenson and Russell Gilmore of The Rifled Arms Historical Association sent me Townsend Whelen's case-forming and loading tools for his .400 to use and take measurements from. These early loading dies are sometimes mistakenly referred to as "Pound Dies." Nothing could be further from the truth. They are not meant to be hit with anything, but instead are to be used in an arbor press. The way Whelen made the cases for the .400 was to neck down cylindrical brass, and I was going to do it the same way. Today there are several sources of cylindrical brass.

With gun and loading tools at hand, but impatient while waiting for brass, I made a die for my lathe to hold annealed .35 Whelen brass. Using a tool that looked like a boring bar with a rounded side I ironed some cases out straight. Using feeler gauges with Whelen's die I found that when the case was .006" from bottoming out I could not force the bolt home on an empty case. At .005" I could get the bolt closed with resistance. No way is a firing pin going to drive this case forward.

I then trimmed the cases to a length of 2.470". When you are using cylindrical brass they are full size out of the die and fire forming is not needed. I dumped in some IMR-3031 topped with a 300gr. DKT round nose bullet. I also loaded a few with the last of my supply of Barnes originals (the ones they no longer make), that shot so well in my .400 Niedner. As luck would have it the Barnes Originals worked much better than the DKT's but in all fairness to DKT I have yet to try their spitzer bullets. A local store did have some of the Barnes X-Bullets .411" diameter in 300gr. so I gave them a try only to shoot a 5' group at 50 yards with them. If I had spent some time doing research on the X-bullets I would have known that they work best when seated .050" off the lands. New loads and back to the range with the X's; results are close to MOA.

The loaner dies of Colonel Whelen's were perfect for the rifle and everything worked great. Dreading the day that I would have to return the dies. I put out the word that I was looking for a set of .400 Whelen dies. A set was located and when I received them I resized a case only to find the dies had reduced the shoulder diameter back to .437". After sending a Cerrosafe cast of the Whelen's dies and two fired cases to RCBS I received a set of dies made perfectly for this rifle. If you have a .400 ANYTHING I suggest that a chamber cast is in order and that .30-06 brass with the .441"shoulder never be used to fire form brass. In one case a person I was corresponding with was having all the problems that I have ever read about with his .400. It turned out he has the original .458" shoulder chambered rifle but his set of dies was for the 06 shoulder.

(Update 10-2000; I just got off the phone with the owner of an early G&H .400 Whelen who is having this exact problem. A quick check of a resized case showed the dies put it back to 06 size.)

How did all this get so mixed up over the passing of time? Did no one ever take the time to measure an early .400 Whelen? One bit of information I have looked for in the early articles written by Whelen was his telling about the larger .458" diameter shoulder. So far I have not found it. Whelen did suggest that only G&H, Hoffman, or Niedner make the .400 Whelen so maybe this was their trade secret. I have cataloged pre-1940 sporters in caliber .400 Whelen made by Griffin & Howe, Fred Adolph, Niedner, Hoffman Arms Co. and Krieghoff of Suhl, Germany. Because of all the bad press many of these rifles have been rebarreled or modified in some way. An early engraved G&H I know of was re-chambered to a belted magnum case so it would have the belt to headspace on.

With the proper chamber and loading dies to match, my rifle has performed flawlessly and is a tribute to Townsend Whelen, James V. Howe and the gunmakers of Griffin & Howe.

.400 Whelen, Part 2

Michael Petrov ©

It was naive of me to think that I could write an article (**PS** February, 2001) for a magazine called ***Precision Shooting*** about a rifle and cartridge and not publish loading information. I received enough inquires about chamber dimensions and loading data that I had to do something. The fact was I wanted to play with this cartridge in a rifle that had a scope; what I did not want to do was modify my little-used Griffin & Howe rifle, so I built a new one. For this project I chose a pre-64 Model 70 Winchester (1951) action and my favorite classic scope, the Lyman Alaskan.

Cartridge	Weight of Bullet grs.	Muzzle Velocity f.s.	Muzzle Energy ft. lbs.	Trajectory 200 yards Height at 100 yds.
25 Special H. P.	86	3300	2080	1.7"
25 Special H. P.	100	3000	1998	1.9
35 Whelen	200	2835	3570	2.5
35 Whelen	250	2635	3855	3.0
400 Whelen	300	2425	3918	3.5

This scope was introduced in 1937. It is a 2½-power scope made with Bausch & Lomb lens, has a 5" eye relief and is perfect for the .400 Whelen. Why this scope was ever discontinued is beyond me. In my opinion this scope will work fine for 90% of all Alaskan hunting. Plus, I think having the windage adjustment in the scope is a handy addition. To explain that, I will say most of my classic custom rifles have the windage adjustment in the mount and this is the most modern rifle and scope combination I own.

In building the new rifle my objective was to duplicate as nearly as possible the original Griffin & Howe rifle. The G&H has a 24" barrel, 1-14" twist and .411" groove diameter. There was no question but that I wanted my friend and gunsmith John Wills to do the work. John is one the most careful workmen I know and everything by him is done right. Word spread fast about the new project and two friends, Dennis P. & Bob Z., wanted a .400 Whelen built as well.

I was delighted to learn that Winchester was reintroducing the .405 Winchester and that Hornady was to make the ammunition as well as the bullets for reloading. I saw my first Hornady bullets made for the .405 at the Shot-Show in Las Vegas 2002 and was relieved to learn that they were .411" in diameter and 300 grain like the originals. What I was not ready for was that they made them with a flat nose. The original bullets had a round nose. The Winchester Model 95 has a box magazine so there is no need for a flat nose. No one at the Hornady Shot-Show booth could tell me why they had a flat nose. In a reply to a follow-up letter to Hornady I was told that the final decision was made by Mr. Hornady with no reason given for the flat nose.

I was surprised at the number of barrel makers who either did not know or had a different idea of what a barrel for the .405 Winchester should be. The original barrels were .411 groove diameter with a 1-14" twist. Luck was on our side because of a call to Shilen, Inc. Not only do they make a textbook barrel, as far as dimensions they had three on hand. My barrel also had to be chrome-moly, I could not justify a custom stock but it would be rust blued, with real wood.

Before we ordered a chambering reamer it was decided that we would have everything on hand such as the barrel, bullets and brass we were going to use. Bob ordered basic brass from Quality Cartridge (PO Box 445, Hollywood, MD 20636) with the .400 Whelen headstamp. I believe this is the first batch in the eighty-year history of the .400 Whelen to have the Whelen headstamp. When the brass arrived I necked some down and trimmed them to length and made several .400 Whelen rounds we could measure. From the loaded ammo and using the measurements from several original .400 Whelen rifles the new reamer was drawn up. The chambering reamer was then ordered from Dave Kiff at Pacific Tool. The chamber was cut for a case with an over all length of 2.501". I adjusted the neck-forming die until the bolt would just close on a case and trimmed it to an OAL of 2.495".

I was determined to do everything by the book and that included following the break-in instructions that came with the barrel. Most of my sporting rifles are fifty to eighty years old and breaking in a barrel was new to me. The new and rebarreled guns I have worked with have all been lead bullet guns where breaking in is not needed. The sheet called for cleaning the barrel after every shot for the first five shots, then cleaning for the next fifty shots after every five shots. "Cleaning the Barrel" means using a bronze brush saturated with solvent making 20 passes through the bore, letting it soak for ten minuets, then saturate the brush for 20 more passes, finishing up by pushing three patches through the barrel to clean it.

I got the original loading data for the .400 Whelen from a *Dupont IMR-3031 pamphlet,* a Griffin & Howe box of loaded ammo and Philip B. Sharpe's *"Complete Guide to Handloading"* all listed 61 grains of 3031 a 300 grain Winchester or WT&C bullet for 2300fps out of a 26" barrel.

The first go round I loaded 58 grains of 3031 and a Hornady 300 grain bullet. Shooting at 50 yards I was amazed to see the very first bullet print, then the next four print lower into a .320" group. I adjusted the scope and got ready for the next fifty rounds of barrel break-in. The brass was well formed and I had no problems other than recoil. I was glad that my project was not a

505 Gibbs. During break-in I tried a couple different powders but from what I could see at 50 yards, 3031 was doing a fine job. H-4895 held a lot of promise and I'm sure if I had worked with it more I could have improved velocity. My intent was to work with the reported velocities circa 1920's. I had no intention of ringing the last FPS out of this cartridge. This is a fine cartridge with a 300-grain bullet at 2260- 2360 fps. Besides I am only shooting at paper bears. If I were to need more I could grab my .400 Niedner, which shoots the same bullet at 2700 fps. I had located a small supply of original Winchester bullets that I loaded to the same specs as G&H used; five-shots at 100 yards into a 1.650" group. If I had a larger supply of these bullets and worked with OAL I'm sure I could have improved on this. I used the RCBS full-length sizing die for sizing down the neck the first time on new brass. After that I necked sized only.

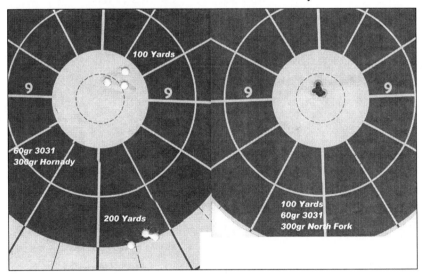

It was apparent right from the start that this rifle likes a cold clean barrel and Hornady bullets. With the barrel and me both broke-in it was time to move to 100 yards. The problem with the Lyman Alaskan 2 ½ power scope at 100 yards is that the cross wire was so big that it covered up the X-Ring of a standard 100-yard target. I had to use 200 yard targets to be able to see some white around the cross wire. Now was the time to try some different bullets. I decided right off that three shot groups should be sufficient for a big-bore hunting rifle. I also was worried that

I would develop a flinch, so I wanted to streamline the bench time as much as possible. My shooting friends did comment that they could not decide which was worse, the report of the .400 Whelen or my whining about the recoil.

Both Dennis and I used pre-64 Model 70 actions originally chambered for the .30-06. Once the actions were barreled and chambered Dennis worked over my original model 70 stock. The barrel channel was relieved and floated approximately .030 -.035 back to the "bell" on the barrel. A channel was milled in the wood directly behind the recoil lug on the receiver to receive a quarter-inch threaded rod. A slot was also milled in the stock directly in front of the trigger slot. A threaded rod was also placed therein. This was done for re-enforcement; Micro-bed™ was used for bedding compound. The milled slots were filled with compound and a small amount of it was placed in the recoil lug slot, under the bell of the barrel, behind the magazine well and the tang area of the stock.

The underside of the rails had to be opened up slightly for the spire-pointed bullets to feed properly, but the Hornadys would come off the left rail and hit the extractor cut in the barrel. This was not a problem for me because the Hornadys are fine for barrel breaking-in and paper punching but with that blunt nose I would always be worried about a failure to feed. Dennis, on the other hand, wanted to shoot them, so John worked on both the rails, feed ramp and the extractor cut until they would feed reliably in his rifle. Bob's rifle was made on a Husqvarna action and only a little work was needed for proper feeding.

I belong to an older school that believed a hunting rifle equipped with a telescope should have a precision adjustable rear sight as well. In Alaska, like other places it can be a long way to the local gunsmith if your scope is broken or damaged. I removed the scope and mounted a Lyman 48, which I then zeroed for this rifle. I can remove the scope, replace the receiver sight slide and be right on target. After I removed the rear sight and remounted the scope I headed back to the range to re-zero the scope. For this I used some of the Hornady bullets and also loaded three cases with the North Fork bullets. I knew the rifle liked a clean cold bore. I wanted to try a three shot group using North Fork bullets with the rifle fouled and the barrel warm. Keeping in mind that the largest group to date (see chart) at 100 yards with NF bullets was .848". After firing several Hornadys the barrel was fouled and warm. I fully expected to see something around an inch or more. Much to my surprise after firing three shots with North Fork bullets all I could see with the 2-1/2-power scope was one black hole that turned out to be a .325" group.

Townsend Whelen wrote in **Wilderness Hunting & Wildcraft** 1927 *"Confidence.-A big-game hunter should have that confidence with his rifle which comes only through perfect familiarity with it."* I can say that I have owned few hunting rifles that I have felt as confident with as I am with this one. It has turned out to be one of the most accurate big-bore rifles I have worked with. It's rewarding to see the first bullet out of a cold and clean barrel go exactly where I place the crosswire. I have a lot of respect for the work of Townsend Whelen. I believe he helped the advancement of the American sporting rifle more than any other single person. The .400 Whelen has for many years been a dark cloud over his name. I hope these two articles have let in a little light.

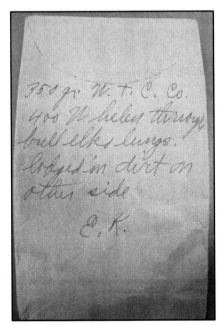

Editor's Note:

Elmer Keith used the 400 Whelen with great success. I recently ran onto a collection of Bullets from Keith's long hunting career. He kept every bullet he could recover and had the details of the kill recorded with them. Several 400 Whelen bullets were included in the collection.

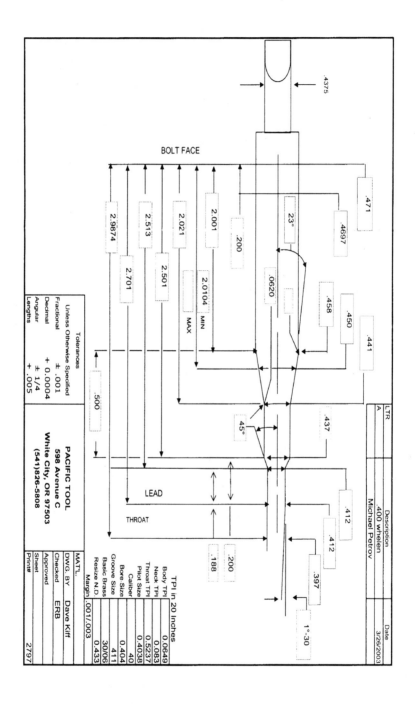

BOLT FACE

.4375

.471

.4697

23°

.200

.0620

.458

.450

.441

2.9874

2.513

2.021

2.001

2.0104 MIN

2.701

2.501

2.0104 MAX

.500

45°

.437

LEAD

THROAT

.412

.412

.397

1°-30

.188

.200

Tolerances
Unless Otherwise Specified
Fractional   ± .001
Decimal   ± 0.0004
Angular   ± 1/4
Lengths   ± .005

PACIFIC TOOL
598 Avenue C
White City, OR 97503
(541)826-5808

LTR			Description	Date
A			.400 whelen	3/26/2003
			Michael Petrov	

TPI in 20 Inches	
Body TPI	0.0649
Neck TPI	0.083
Throat TPI	0.5237
Pilot Size	0.4038
Caliber	40
Bore Size	0.404
Groove Size	411
Basic Brass	30/06
Resize N.D.	0.433
Margin	.0011/.003

MATL.		
DWG. BY		Dave Kiff
Checked		ERB
Approved		
Sheet		
Print#		2797

62

.400 Whelen 24" Barrel						
Bullet	**Bullet**	**Powder**	**Powder**	**Average**	**Range**	**3-Shot**
Make	**Weight**	**Type**	**Weight**	**Velocity**	**Yards**	**Group**
Hornady	300	IMR-3031	60	2260	200	1.080"
Hornady	300	IMR-3031	60	2260	100	0.415"
Hornady	300	IMR-3031	62	2337		
Winchester	300	IMR-3031	61	2260	100	
Hawk	300	IMR-3031	60	2210	100	0.960"
Barnes X	300	IMR-3031	56	2040		
North Fork	300	IMR-3031	60	2385	100	0.400"
North Fork	300	IMR-3031	60	2385	100	0.482"
North Fork	300	IMR-3031	60	2385	100	0.618"
North Fork	300	IMR-3031	60	2385	100	0.848"
Hornady	300	H-4895	60	2543	100	1.145"
Hornady	300	IMR-3031	60	2282	100	0.971"
Hornady	300	H-4895	61		50	0.341"
North Fork	300	IMR-3031	60	2362	100	0.325"

WARNING! This loading data is for **Petrov's** Winchester Model 70 only! There are so many incorrectly chambered .400 Whelen rifles or dies that reduce the shoulder diameter you need to make sure what you have before you proceed.

These articles about the 400 Whelen originally appeared in Precision Shooting Magazine, February, 2001 issue and the December, 2003 issue. Thanks to Michael Petrov for all his research, and willingness to share it with the shooting fraternity.

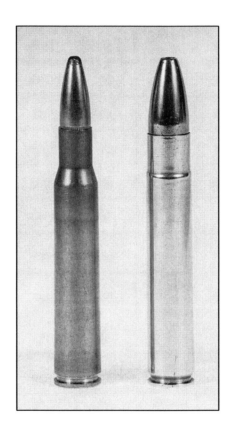

30-06 vs. 411 Hawk

Or

30-06 On Steroids!

Z Rule of 3

The table below is based on the premise that with modern cartridges, generally operating at velocities between 2500 and 3200 feet per second. Zeroing a scope-sighted hunting rifle so that bullet impact at one hundred yards is above point of aim gives practical peak effectiveness for both rifle and cartridge. By doing this the rifle is zeroed for a range between two and three hundred yards, the precise range depending on velocity, bullet weight, and shape of the bullet.

The bullet rises no more than three inches above line of sight, drops back through that line, and by the time it has dropped three inches below the line of sight has reached a range close to the maximum distance for proper expansion of many bullets today. That maximum range is the effective "point blank range." We can hold dead on our game to that distance, since the bullet will rise and fall only three inches off our line of sight. In practical big game hunting the animal's vital area is at least six inches in diameter. Only the practiced shooter can hold inside six inches beyond a furlong (220 yards) anyway. But as a practiced shooter, you know that already.

The table has been carried out to give the range at which we should hold over 10 inches, which is to say on the back line or withers line of game animals like deer, elk, antelope. For most modern loads the 10 inch holdover distance is between 250 and 400 yards, to accurately judge greater distances you should probably use a laser range finder. Besides, an old timer once told me that, "you should always aim at hair." Advice that has proven to be true many times over.

To use the table, zero your rifle for hunting to hit the listed point of impact at 100 yards, this is of course done by aiming at the center of the target. Then memorize only the "Maximum Point Blank Range" and "10 inch Holdover" yardages for that load. Forget other trajectory factors as merely confusing. If your pet cartridge is not listed, pick the one nearest to it in velocity and bullet weight, adjusting the yardage: slightly as the relative speeds indicate. In other words, for the 180-grain .308 Winchester load, use the 180 grain .30-06 data and reduce the ranges by 10-20 yards, not enough to upset matters when you are shooting under hunting conditions. These days chronographs are cheap enough that any serious shooter can afford one, then you can work out your specific trajectory.

Z-Hat Custom, Rule of 3 Table

Cartridge / Bullet Wt.	Velocity Feet Per Second	Point of impact @ 100 yards	Trajectory Peak in Yards	Target "zero" in Yards	Maximum Point Blank Range in Yards	10" Holdover in Yards
17 Remington 25gr.	4040	+2.16	165	287	331	395
22 Hornet 45gr.	2690	+2.93	112	190	219	265
22-250 55gr.	3680	+2.33	158	269	310	375
243 Winchester 100gr.	2960	+2.63	138	243	284	348
240 Hawk 100gr.	3867	+2.06	179	316	370	455
25-06 115gr.	2990	+2.6	141	247	290	355
260 Remington 140gr.	2750	+2.75	130	228	268	330
264 Hawk 140gr.	2970	+2.59	143	251	295	362
264 Winchester 140gr.	3030	+2.58	142	250	293	359
270 Winchester 130gr.	3050	+2.84	123	216	253	312
7mm-08 140g.	2800	+2.7	134	238	279	348
280 Hawk 160gr.	2992	+2.58	143	251	295	365

Cartridge / Bullet Wt.	Velocity Feet Per Second	Point of impact @ 100 yards	Trajectory Peak in Yards	Target "zero" in Yards	Maximum Point Blank Range in Yards	10" Holdover in Yards
7mm Remington 175gr.	2850	+2.67	136	240	282	347
30-30 Win. 150gr.	2390	+2.98	106	182	211	258
30-06 180gr.	2700	+2.79	127	223	261	322
300 Hawk 180gr.	2887	+2.59	141	251	294	364
3200 Hawk 150gr.	3200	+2.52	146	254	296	362
338 Hawk 225gr.	2759	+2.74	130	230	269	332
338 Win. 225gr.	2920	+2.64	138	242	284	349
35 Whelen 200gr.	2675	+2.83	123	215	251	316
358 Hawk 200gr.	2820	+2.75	130	225	263	326
9.3x62 286gr.	2362	+2.95	111	195	229	282
375Hawk/Scovill 250gr.	2701	+2.79	127	223	262	321
375 H&H 300gr.	2530	+2.87	120	212	248	307
411 Hawk 300gr.	2550	+2.88	118	208	243	298
416 Remington 400gr.	2400	+2.93	114	201	235	288
458 Win. 500gr.	2120	+3	98	173	203	247

The load data in this table is derived from published factory load data for the specific cartridges. In the case of Hawk cartridges we used data directly from Z-Hat Custom's load data. Sights are assumed to be 1.5" above the center of bore for these tables, as most scopes are at this height.

There is a trend toward longer range shooting with Ultra velocity cartridges these days. If that is your area of interest check out the second chart below for Ultra velocity cases (those which far exceed the velocity of the cartridges listed in the first table). Check your velocity and it's a simple matter to figure your "Point Blank Range." This system is simple and practical, it works.

Z-Hat Custom, Rule of 3, Table # 2

Cartridge/ Bullet Wt.	Velocity Feet Per Second	Point of Impact @ 100 yards	Trajectory Peak in Yards	Target "zero" in Yards	Maximum Point Blank Range in Yards	10" Holdover in Yards
240 Weatherby 87gr.	3523	+2.31	161	281	328	402
240 Hawk 80gr.	4000	+2.04	181	314	366	445
257 Hawk 115gr.	3890	+2.07	179	314	367	450
270 WSM 130gr.	3275	+2.84	123	216	253	312
270 Weatherby 140gr.	3300	+2.39	156	275	323	397
7mm STW 160gr.	3325	+2.4	155	272	318	391
300 Rem. Ultra 180gr.	3250	+2.45	152	265	310	379
338-378 Wby 250gr.	3060	+2.54	145	257	302	373
375 Rem. Ultra 300gr.	2760	+2.74	130	230	269	334
416 Weatherby 400gr.	2700	+2.8	125	219	256	315
460 Weatherby 500gr.	2600	+2.87	120	210	245	299

The load data in this table is derived from published factory load data for the specific cartridges. In the case of Hawk cartridges we used data directly from Z-Hat Custom's published load data. Sights are assumed to be 1.5" above the center of bore for these tables, as most scopes are at this height.

Powder Profiles for "411 Hawk"

Mike Brady

For the last couple of years, I have been intrigued with the 411 Hawk cartridge that brought to commercial fruition by Fred Zeglin of Z-Hat Custom. Ever since the introduction of the cartridge, back in about 1997, I have considered chambering a Model 95 Browning/USRAC/Winchester in 411 Hawk. My combined interest in the rifle, and cartridge lead to extensive testing of the cartridge far beyond that required for the R&D of the bullets that we manufacture in that caliber at North Fork Bullets. All of the testing has been to satisfy one ulterior motive... I WANT ONE.

Although the original intent of Fred may have been to produce the largest and most powerful cartridge that could be based on the -06 case, my goals were a little more conservative because I already had the M95 in mind. There is no doubt that the M95 Browning or USRAC/Winchester is capable of withstanding the SAAMI designated maximum pressures of 60,000 psi. The factory has cambered the 95 for cartridges like 270 Winchester, which is arguably the hottest factory loaded cartridge on the 06 case. Since the action is a rear lockup design, and for purely personal reasons, I decided to stay well clear of those pressures that are I feel are better suited to bolt guns.

My specific parameters for a M95 and 411Hawk project are listed below.

1)   Max OAL of 3.250" to fit the M95 magazine

2)   300gr bullet at 2500 fps from a 24" barrel

3)   325gr bullet at 2375 fps from a 24" barrel

4)   Both the above velocities achieved at a MAP of 52,000 to 53,000psi (7 to 8 thousand psi less than the parent cartridges) and no variations exceeding 54,000psi

All pressure/velocity data was collected using an Oehler M43PBL; therefore all pressures in this text are in PSI (M43). The test rifle used for the pressure data was supplied by Fred Zeglin and was based on a Model 98 Mauser fitted with a 25" Douglas barrel. Additional, velocity only, data was collected from a M95 takedown with a 24" barrel, only after specific loads were analyzed in the pressure gun. The accompanying data was collected using bullets manufactured by North Fork Technologies, Inc..

The substitution of bullets from other manufacturers or any other components different than those listed, could produce dangerously high pressures. At the very least, any substitutions would render the load/velocity/pressure data useless. All loads were safe in the rifles they were tested in but that does not mean they would be safe in all rifles so chambered. Reduce all loads 10% and adjust accordingly while keeping an eye toward signs of excessive pressure.

All references as to powders chosen, case capacities, and drop tube usage, may very well be due to the specific design of North Fork bullets and may or may not apply to products of other manufacturers.

Powders

Due to the limited case capacity (considering the bullet caliber and weight) of this cartridge, virtually all top loads required the use of a 24" drop tube. This is because the North Fork bullets is longer than the average bullet due to it's design.

IMR3031

Due to the long grain nature of this powder, it does not yield any significant increase in capacity with the use of a drop tube. That coupled with my aversion to compressing powders that give off a sound akin to stepping on corn flakes, it becomes apparent that the 4l1 Hawk does not have sufficient capacity to utilize 3031 for top loads. Although not adequate for top loads, 3031 loaded to 100% density behind the 300gr bullet will yield better than 405

Winchester ballistics, at very modest pressures.

NF 300gr 57.0gr IMR3031 = 2275 @ 43,100psi

IMR4198

Other than for fire forming (more on that later), this powder is much too fast for anything other than low velocity and/or cast bullet loads.

Alliant RE 7

Considering the lack of capacity for proper use of 3031 as well as past experience with both powders, I had high hopes for RE-7. Unfortunately, this powder produces velocities a full 150 fps behind the better powders when loaded to equivalent pressures of 52 to 53K psi. It still falls short by 50 to 100 fps even when loaded to max pressures for a bolt gun of over 60,000 psi.

There is another strange phenomenon that occurs with the use of this powder in this cartridge. Regardless of all the excellent articles warning against the use of appearance of spent primers as an indicator of pressure, it is still the most used indicator by the average handloader. It's the old (the primers not as flat as a pancake, so I can put in one more grain!) syndrome. With this powder, in this cartridge, that could prove to be hazardous to your health. The appearance of the spent primer, no matter what brand or type, used to ignite this powder seems to indicate pressures much below what is actually happening. This has not happened with any other powder tried. Even loads in excess of 60,000 psi produce a primer appearance similar to a 30.000 psi cast bullet load. No doubt that this phenomenon may come from the use of particular components of certain lot numbers, but it happens all too frequently to ignore. Considering the poor pressure/velocity relationship, coupled with the strange primer appearance, I cannot recommend this powder in this cartridge.

NF 300 gr   55.0 gr   RE 7 = 2388 @ 52,400 psi

NF 300 gr   57.0 gr   RE 7 = 2467 @ 59,600 psi

NF 325 gr   54.0 gr   RE 7 = 2317 @ 60,600 psi

Hogdon H322

This powder acts, in this cartridge, just like a ball powder version of RE 7 (but it doesn't do anything weird to the primers). Pressures mount rapidly and it always falls short of velocities produced by the better powders. Not recommended in the 411 Hawk.

Hogdon Varget

In this cartridge, Varget acts very similar to H-4895, maybe just a tad slower. What can be said of one can be said of the other.

NF 300 gr   64.0 gr   Varget = 2425 @ 48,200 psi (Max with comp.)

NF 300 gr   62.0 gr   Varget = 2394 @ 47,500 psi (Max w/o comp.)

Alliant RE 12

The limited case capacity of the 411 Hawk will not allow full utilization of RE-12. It appears to generate just a little more pressure for the same velocity as 3031. It would still be useful for 405 Winchester ballistics and may (along with all the slower powders) have use with other manufacturers bullets, especially in the heavier weights.

NF 325 gr 58.0 gr RE 12 = 2187 @ 41,600 psi

NF 325 gr 62.0 gr RE 12 = 2324 @ 49,500 psi

(Max, drop tube plus camp.)

Hogdon H335

This powder is dense enough to fit in the 411 case and reach bolt gun pressures of 60,000 psi but the velocities generated do not justify the wear and tear. In fact BL-C(2) will develop the same velocities at 4 to 6K psi less pressure, so what's the point. Aside from the poor pressure/velocity relationship, another peculiar effect manifests itself with this powder (and to a lesser degree with all ball powders). At max pressures, the bullet is bumped up in the bore so hard that the grooves of the North Fork Bullet can be ironed out, which negates the antifouling purpose of the grooves. Also the base of the bullet becomes cup shaped and appears to have been shot in the butt with a load of buckshot. This phenomenon has never occurred with any extruded powder, even at blue pill pressures. All ball powders do this to some extent, but H-335 offered the most pronounced results. The distortion starts to occur at 55,000 psi and is severe at 60,000 psi. This is all happening to a solid copper base so you can imagine what would happen to a full lead cored bullet. Due to the distortion and unfavorable pressure/velocity relationship, this powder is not recommended in the 411 Hawk.

NF 325 gr 62.0 gr H-335 = 2325 @ 50,800 psi

NF 325 gr 64.0 gr H-335 = 2400 @ 55,000 psi (distortion begins)
NF 325 gr 65.0 gr H-335 = 2431 @ 59,900 psi (distortion severe)

Alliant RE 15

This powder is much too slow for the lighter bullet weights but some preliminary tests have shown possible use with 400 gr bullets. Sample shots indicated velocities in the area of 450/400 and 404 Jeffery, albeit at top bolt gun pressures.

BL-C 2

The hands down winner in the powder pageant (at least with North Fork bullets) has been Hogdon's BL-C(2). This powder showed the best pressure/velocity relationship (highest velocity for the lowest pressure) over any other powder tried. Being a ball powder, the use of the drop tube allows an extra five grains of powder to be used without compressing the powder charge; top loads running from 98% to 100% density. If all other variables are kept constant it also delivers a very low standard of deviation. Once BL-C(2) was found to be the best powder I had access to, data was generated with the M43 using different powder charges and different primers to find the best combination to satisfy the original parameters of the M95 4ll Hawk project.

Like most pageant winners, if you take a long look you will find a blemish, BL-C(2) produces a noticeable muzzle flash. This flash is so strong that most hunters will not like this powder in the 411 Hawk as it will blind you in low light conditions normally expected when hunting.

H4895

The second best powder behind BL-C(2) was H-4895. It has a similar pressure/velocity relationship and velocities very close to (but still short of) BL-C(2) can be achieved but only by compressing the powder in conjunction with the drop tube, which I do not like to do. Without compression, velocities will run 50 to 100 fps behind BL-C(2) with a corresponding reduction in pressure. All in all, a very good powder if you are willing to accept the reduced velocity. Max capacity loads:

NF 300gr 64.0 gr. H-4895 = 2493 @ 49,200 psi

NF 325gr 62.0 gr. H-4895 = 2400 @ 51,800 psi

Powders Not Tried

Other powders that may have application are AC 2015BR, AC 2230, AC 2460, AC 2495BR, Norma 201, Win 748, IMR 4064, IMR 4895, Viht N133, and Viht N135. The ones that appear to be the most interesting are 2015 BR (works well in 416 Rem and 458 Win), 2495BR (said to be close to 4895), and Win 748. I'm still looking for an extruded powder that will best BL-C(2) but I haven't found it yet.

Primers

The primers that were tried were those that were on hand. Generally most of my experimentation is done with CCI 200 primers but with this cartridge I also added CCI 250 and the Fed 215.

The purpose of adding the magnum primers was to see if they would

- Increase velocities with the limited powder space
- Reduce standard deviation through more complete combustion
- Reduce the onerous muzzle flash produced by ball powders

In comparing the CCI200 and the CCI 250, there did not seem to be any marked improvement with the 250 over the 200; in fact there seemed to be very little difference between the two as far as pressure, velocity, or anything else.

In trying the Fed 215, it was interesting and curious to find that it (with all else equal) produced less velocity and pressure than the CCI 200. The difference wasn't much, on the order of 2,000 psi, (equivalent to a .5 gr. difference in powder charge) but it was definite and repeatable. I have seen others try to explain the peculiarity of a supposedly "hotter" primer producing lower velocities and pressures but all I know is the cause is just theory but the effect is fact.

One other fact should be pointed out as to the physical differences between the Federal and CCI primers. The CCI primers seem to be made of either a stronger or thicker material than the Federal primers. This has been noticed over several different lot numbers of both brands. The Federal primers seat with less force and flatten more, upon firing, than the CCI primers. The CCI primer will not flatten until very excessive pressures are reached. The Federal primers will flatten out, to what appears to be factory pressure levels, at much less than factory levels. This is not to say that either primer should be preferred over the other for this reason alone, the difference just needs to be recognized.

In the 4ll Hawk tests, the Federal primer worked very well but the primers appeared to indicate pressures higher than the strain gauge indicated and the appearance of the CCI primers, which worked equally well, indicated just the reverse. As has always been the case, primer appearance is near to useless in ascertaining pressure levels. As far as standard deviation, I would give a very slight nod to the Fed 215 but the difference is so small that I would certainly not run out and buy Federals when I had a drawer full of CCIs. Neither magnum primer was effective in reducing the ball powder muzzle flash.

Mikes thoughts on the 411 Hawk...

The 411 Hawk is a very straight forward and hassle free cartridge. The one trait that seems to be a little more exaggerated than in other cartridges is variations in pressure and velocity due to differences in neck tension. All casings that were used were from the same bag and lot number and they were fire formed in the same fashion using the same load and procedures. (Only the first full load, after the fireform load, was used for pressure tests.) Even so, differing neck tensions were noted at the seating of the bullet. Toward the end of the experiments it became very easy to predict which cartridges in a string would be the higher and lower velocity (and pressure) shots, with virtually 100% regularity. This may be nit picking because we are talking about a standard deviation of 5 with equal neck tensions and 15 without, but this is the first cartridge that I have worked with that 90+% of the variations can so easily be attributed to one specific cause. (Actually, I don't consider the fact that variations can be traced to one source as a negative; solve one small problem and you've got yourself a Camp Perry elephant gun).

It can even be seen on the M43 data sheets that some loads with lesser powder charges produced higher velocities and pressures; this was in fact due to neck tension alone, and was predicted at the time of bullet seating. Also, for whatever reason, the cases that were fire formed in the M95, for the most part, had a good, strong, and even tension which would explain why a gun with a shorter barrel produced velocities equal to or greater than the pressure gun, again predicted at the time of seating. Maybe this stronger tension was due to the rifle they were fire formed in or maybe it was just the luck of the draw when I pulled the virgin casings out of the bag. Normally this situation would have indicated the use of a crimp but the die I was using did not have that capability. A test for another time. Since Z-Hat has started carrying Lee factory crimp dies for the 411 Hawk to help shooters easily deal with neck tension.

It's possible that this situation could be improved somewhat by reducing the neck to a smaller dimension in the sizer die but the basic problem is not caused by the die but rather by variations in the brass. If the die had been the culprit, all the brass would be the same, either loose or snug, but not both. If the die dimension was reduced, the variation would then be between snug and very snug, but it would still be there. It must be stated that I was working with an early handmade (not from current production machinery) die and Fred reports no similar peculiarities have occurred with current manufactured dies. Even so, I still don't think it is a die problem.

Another possible solution may be to neck anneal, although all the casings formed well, without any failures, as is. (Possibly anneal after the fireform?) It also may very well be that this situation will vanish with multiple firings, as the necks become work hardened to an equal degree. This test was not conducted because pressure data becomes more suspect as the casing is subjected to multiple firings. Actually, pressure tests on multiple fired cases would not be necessary because if the seating force and therefore the neck tensions felt equal, then the problem is solved. You will know it when you feel it.

Fireforming

Due to comments directed to Z-Hat about fireforming loads using inexpensive 41 caliber pistol bullets and my own growing aversion to burning up expensive hunting bullets just to fireform, I decided to investigate the practicality of their use. From our accumulated experience (Fred & myself) it was known that the shoulder would not form adequately with anything much less than a full load; definitely not with a light load. I wanted to find the lowest pressure that would form a shoulder that would serve it's intended purpose.

You will seldom get a fully defined, sharp shoulder until the second or third hunting load anyway so don't strain your gun trying to get it on the first shot. I decided to use a Hornady 210 gr silhouette bullet. The theory here was that the more or less full metal jacket design would more likely withstand the high velocities needed to generate the pressures required, without coming apart in flight. Soft or hollow point bullets may also work but I didn't wish to take the chance. I originally chose IMR 4198 because with so light of a bullet, a fast powder would be required to generate sufficient pressures. It worked so well that I saw no reason to experiment with other powders. The chart below shows the results.

Hornaday 210 Silhouette using IMR 4198 and CCI 200 primer. Bullet seated to cannelure.

40.0   gr = 2246 @ 30,500 psi (insufficient pressure)

45.0   gr = 2447 @ 33,800 psi (insufficient pressure)

50.0   gr = 2627 @ 37,700 psi (insufficient pressure)

55.0   gr = 2859 @ 51,400 psi (adequate reliable shoulder)

The 55.0 gr load was tried several times and proved to be very consistent. Velocity was 2860 +or- 10 fps and pressure was 52,000 +or- 1,000 psi.

A secondary benefit to the experiment was that the little Hornaday bullet may have some hunting applications if the quarry is 150 pounds or less and the launch speeds are kept to 2350 fps (42.0 gr 4198) or less. Don't let that semi full metal jacket fool you, they open like lightning. No controlled expansion here, they flatten like a penny on a railroad track. Considering the abuse of impacting at twice their designed velocity, they hold their weight surprisingly well. Penetration is only a little more than a third of a serious hunting bullet but an antelope or a scrawny Mississippi whitetail wouldn't know the difference. Pick the speed up to 2600 fps and it would make quite a rock chuck hand grenade. (I have no use for a one season gun).

Just follow Z-Hat's instructions on forming the shoulder for the 411 Hawk, seat the bullet to the cannelure over the 55.0 gr load and shoot. When you seat the bullet the temporary shoulder may look a little lopsided, more shoulder on one side than the other, but this seems to make no difference in the outcome. The shoulder derived from this load is fully capable of doing it's intended duty.

As to the reliability of the shoulder on this cartridge, let me say that I have never experienced any squibs, hang fires, misfires, or any other aberration indicating anything other than perfect and reliable ignition. Anyone who reports difficulties with this cartridge likely did not read the fire forming instructions provided with their gun.

M95 Observations

My criterion for success of the designed loads in the M95 was that when they were fired in the gun there would be minimal case stretching. This would indicate that the chosen working pressures were conducive to less stress on the gun as well as long case life. The best loads (that fit the chosen parameters) of both the 300 and 325 grain bullets, as ascertained from the pressure gun, were then fired in the M95. Measurements of the fired cases indicated zero case stretching, so the tests were deemed successful and were concluded.

When using North Fork bullets and BL-C(2), my recommendations are to choose the other components that you desire, reduce the listed loads by 5% and work up until a velocity of 2500 to 2525 fps is achieved with the 300 gr. bullet. 2375 to 2400 fps is achieved with the 325 gr. bullet. In this way the maximum safe velocities will be achieved according to the original parameters that were set down.

Michael L. Brady, Founder

North Fork Tech., Inc

ALWAYS WERE SAFETY GLASSES AND HEARING PROTECTION WHEN RELOADING OR SHOOTING.

If you are unfamiliar with the terminology and processes described here we recommend that you read any or all of the following; Nick Harvey's Practical Reloading Manual, Handbook for Shooters & Reloaders Vol. I & II by P.O. Ackley, Designing & Forming Custom Cartridges by Ken Howell, or just about any brand name reloading manual will contain the information you need to be a safe reloader.

PART II Load Data

19 Hawk

During the writing of Fred Zeglin's book, "Wildcat Cartridges, Reloader's Handbook of Wildcat Cartridge Design" the idea for a 19 caliber cartridge was born. The history of the 219 Donaldson Wasp played a large roll in the design of the 19 Hawk. Donaldson literally spent years perfecting his design for the 219 Wasp. His stated goals according to Samuel Clark, Jr., in "Twenty-Two Caliber Varmint Rifles" by Charles S. Landis, 1946, were as follows, "It was not the idea of "improving" any particular cartridge but more that of

19 Hawk Chamber

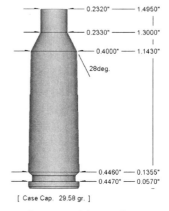

[Case Cap. 29.58 gr.]

producing a small, convenient, high intensity cartridge of great accuracy, economy and very flat trajectory without going to the realm of long, heavy cases which often gave high erosion and, at times, considerable pressures near the head. The line of thought was practical, at least when used with a moderate degree of throating."

Fred looked at the case capacity in relation to the bore and with the idea of making a 19 Hawk started looking for an appropriate case. There were a few factors to consider, first and foremost was the need for a cartridge that would work in a commonly available gun. Second, was a case that would have similar case capacity to it's grandfather, the 219 Donaldson Wasp in relation to the smaller bore diameter of the 19. Ultimately the 7.32x39 case was selected because it required a minimal amount of reforming to provide a cartridge that had the capacity desired.

Winchester was making brass so availability and cost would not be a problem. You might ask why not use the 22 PPC case?

Simply, 22 PPC brass is more expensive and harder to locate than 7.62x39 brass so it does not meet the criteria of convenience and economy. Also the 22 PPC would require substantial reforming to reduce case capacity.

For those of you who are always looking for more velocity, a 19 PPC would be the equivalent of an improved 19 Hawk. Many varmint shooters are looking for small calibers with low recoil, relatively low report, and accuracy. The 19 Hawk meets all these qualifications. We recorded groups averaging .200's during testing, further experimenting will be done with different throat lengths, and a 20 caliber version will be developed too.

If you see the velocities below as less than you expected, keep in mind the goal in developing this cartridge was an accurate cartridge with varmint applications. Consequently we did not feel the need to seek maximum velocities, we loaded for accuracy, as the target below indicates.

19 Hawk, 36 gr. Calhoon
.187" group
@100 Yards

Bullet Mfg	Bullet Wgt.	Style	Load OAL
Calhoon	36	HP	1.945

Primer	Powder	Powder Wgt. Gr.	Velocity
CCI 200	N 540	24	3312
CCI 200	N 540	24.5	3442 *
CCI 200	N 540	25	3553
CCI 200	IMR 4895	24	3355
CCI 200	IMR 4064	24	3491
CCI 200	IMR 4064	24.5	3568
CCI 200	RL 15	23.5	3536
CCI 200	H380	25	3357
CCI 200	H380	26	3452
CCI 200	BLC2	24	3257
CCI 200	BLC2	25	3368
CCI 200	H322	24	3719

* most accurate load tested

Bullet Mfg	Bullet Wgt.	Style	Load OAL
Calhoon	40	HP	1.940"

Primer	Powder	Powder Wgt. Gr.	Velocity
CCI 200	IMR 4064	24.5	3544
CCI 200	N 540	24	3355
CCI 200	N 540	24.1	3360 *
CCI 200	N 540	24.5	3410
CCI 200	H322	23.5	3564

*

most accurate load tested

Bullet Mfg	Bullet Wgt.	Style	Load OAL
Calhoon	44	HP	1.945"

Primer	Powder	Powder Wgt. Gr.	Velocity
CCI 200	H380	24	3082
CCI 200	H380	25	3201
CCI 200	IMR 4350	25	3072
CCI 200	IMR 4350	25.5	3076
CCI 200	IMR 4350	26	3182
CCI 200	IMR 4350	26.5	3242
CCI 200	IMR 4064	24	3447
CCI 200	IMR 4320	25	3473
CCI 200	N 540	23.5	3277 *
CCI 200	N 540	24	3340

* most accurate load tested

Brass Selection for Hawk Cartridges
From 240 through 3200

Headspacing for this group of cartridges require only one gage set, I did not want to have separate gages for each caliber, that would be a waste of money. By utilizing 280 Remington brass I was able to give these "smaller" Hawk Cartridges greater capacity, thus producing better velocity without the need for excessive pressures. I use a standard or traditional 280 Rem. AI go gage to headspace for the smaller Hawk Cartridges.

There was a fair amount of buzz among Ackley fans when Nosler decided to take the 280 Ackley to SAAMI in 2006. Nosler wanted to pay Ackley the honor of using his name, they even called the Ackley family and asked permission to use the name as a courtesy, both are admirable acts. While it's not all that unusual for a company to legitimize a wildcat, it is, with few exceptions, unusual for the cartridge to retain the designers original name. There is a reason for this, whenever a factory decides to bring a wildcat to commercial production they are concerned about the fact that many gunsmiths will copy a wildcat, but, are not diligent about headspacing it as it was designed.

Headspace is probably the least understood and at the same time simplest of mechanical concepts. Simply put, proper headspacing insures that the case head will be held tight against the bolt face so that the cartridge can be safely fired. This definition will suffice for the purposes of this discussion.

When Nosler contemplated the idea of bringing a fifty-something year old wildcat to the industry as a factory offering they, looked around the see how the cartridge had been treated during its history. Many gunsmiths are vague on the proper headspace for an Ackley Improved bottle-neck cartridge. All you do is use the Ackley go gauge and use the standard go gauge for caliber as the

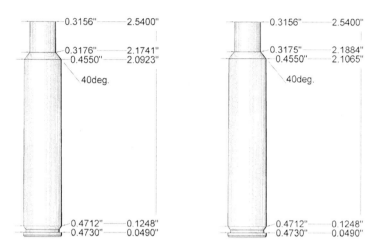

no-go. i.e. Use a 280 AI go gauge with a 280 Remington go gauge as the no-go. Ackley knew what he was doing, here's the proof, the difference in length between the two gauges just mentioned is .004" (4/1000 of an inch). The difference between a standard 280 Remington go gauge and no-go gage is .004". So when you chamber a factory 280 case in a 280 AI chamber it is crushed at the point where the neck and the shoulder meet. This crush holds the case tight against the bolt face for fire forming.

All sounds pretty simple, right? Well, apparently not.

Many gunsmiths fail to follow this simple formula. So, their Ackley or in this case Hawk chambers may be too long or too short depending on how they misapply the headspace gauges. To complicate matters further, Nosler found out that Remington's custom shop had been setting the headspace on their 280 Ackley Improved chambers .014" shorter than the Ackley standard.

Research turned up nobody who was willing to go on record as to the logic behind changing specifications for an established cartridge with a long history and large amounts of published data. To further complicate the discussion some headspace gages are made with the 40 degree shoulder and others as Ackley intended with the original 18° shoulder angle.

Most wildcatters, and for that matter reamer makers, subscribe to a policy that if you change the dimensions for a cartridge you must clearly mark those changes on the reamer or firearm, or better yet rename the cartridge to avoid confusion. Even Ken Green at SAAMI says that, "If the industry is going to mine the field of wildcats and CIP cartridges, we should use them as designed or change the name." SAAMI has no veto power over its members if they decide to offer a cartridge in any given configuration, the decisions are made by a vote of the member companies.

Lets try an analogy, you stop at the bakery to pick up some fresh danish on your way to work. The danish all look different from shelf to shelf, you order a dozen cheese danish and the baker fills a box for you. When you arrive at work and open the box you find there are no two danish alike in the box, calling the bakery your told they are all "cheese" danish. Co-workers ask what you brought, you say cheese danish, soon they are all gone.

In no time your co-workers are telling you that they were not cheese danish at all and each had a different flavor. Worst of all one co-worker is deathly allergic to almonds and they received a danish filled with almond paste. Just one bite sends them off to the hospital and they may not survive.

Calling the bakery again to tell them what happened, the baker laughs at you and says, "You should have known we changed the recipe on all of our "cheese" danish. None of them contain any cream cheese, that's old fashioned thinking, what's in a name?"

A stretch? Sure. Yet, changing cartridge specifications is fairly common, mainly because of poor gunsmith practices, and apparently sometimes when engineers think they "know better" than the original designer. Back to our 280 Ackley Improved...

Nosler, SAAMI, and indirectly Remington all site headspace as the reason for the shorter than standard headspace.

The idea being, if someone fire-forms using factory 280 Remington brass or ammo it will hold the case head tight to the bolt face. How is that better than the original design that did the same thing? OK, it will work...

Now the problem, if I have a 280 Ackley Improved chambered exactly to the specifications that P.O. Ackley set forth and I unwittingly buy some of the 280 AI Nosler brass I will have, misfires, poor accuracy, stretched brass, short brass life, case head separations or any combination there of.

All the conditions described in the previous chapter can be caused by excessive headspace. That's right, your gun can be correctly headspaced and the brass can still cause headspace problems. Nosler brass is made to match the SAAMI dimensions. If your a gunsmith building a rifle in 280 AI be sure to ask your customer if they plan to use Nosler brass or which gage is preferred by your client, "Ackley" or "SAAMI," otherwise you or your client will likely be subject to an allergic reaction.

Hawk cartridges <u>cannot</u> utilize 280 AI Nosler brass.

ALWAYS WERE SAFETY GLASSES AND HEARING PROTECTION WHEN RELOADING OR SHOOTING.

If you are unfamiliar with the terminology and processes described here we recommend that you read any or all of the following; Nick Harvey's Practical Reloading Manual, Handbook for Shooters & Reloaders Vol. I & II by P.O. Ackley, Designing & Forming Custom Cartridges by Ken Howell, or just about any brand name reloading manual will contain the information you need to be a safe reloader.

Hawk Cartridges; Forming Instructions.

240 Hawk through 3200 Hawk.

For your safety and convenience we recommend that you use only new unfired brass, all from one manufacturers lot number. 280 Remington brass works the best for these calibers because they are slightly longer than the parent 30-06 case, and the cartridges were designed to use the 280 case. 06 brass will work but usually runs shorter in overall length, special instructions for 30-06 brass are provided below as well.

Starting with 280 Remington brass, size the neck of your cases to the new diameter. Check the unprimed empty brass to be sure it headspaces properly. At this point you will want to have your rifle handy, check the cases for proper fit in the chamber. The bolt should close on the brass without undue force, but you should feel the bolt drag on the brass as it closes. Once this setting is located lock your size die lock ring to prevent changes. Recheck each piece of sized brass for proper fit. If you're sizing up, the 300 Hawk should be a simple matter of using the standard expander ball in your size die to open the neck. If you're going up to 3200 Hawk, you will need a tapered expander ball to avoid collapsing necks.

Otherwise simply set up the sizing die as you would with any standard caliber and size the cases.

Minimum trim lengths are as follows;

240 Hawk, 2.475"	270 Hawk, 2.475"	3200 Hawk, 2.475"
257 Hawk, 2.475"	284 Hawk, 2.475"	(Maximum length is
264 Hawk, 2.475"	300 Hawk, 2.475"	.010" longer)

30-06 Brass: When utilizing 30-06 brass for calibers 270 and smaller follow the sizing directions above to create the false shoulder described below. For 284 and up you will need to expand the neck of the brass to a diameter larger than the final

89

caliber, before sizing (two calibers is best). Then size the neck in your Hawk die.

This process will create a "false shoulder," so called because the case will look like it has two shoulders, Figure 1. The original shoulder will still be there and a new shoulder will appear where the size die stops on the neck. The cartridge will then headspace on this new shoulder.

Figure 1.

Congratulations, that is all there is to it.

Now just, prime, and load as usual, with the components of your choice, and fire form. You will want to trim to length after fire forming as the process will affect the neck length. Wear safety glasses when reloading and be safe.

Brass Selection for Hawk Cartridges
From 338 through 411

Headspacing for this group of cartridges is accomplished with one set of gages. Because these larger calibers have a 17 degree 30 minute shoulder they have their own gages. The only real difference between this medium to large caliber group is the shoulder angle, and that is why a separate set of gages is required.

My personal choice to form these wildcats is 35 Whelen brass from Remington. It is easy to form and saves time over necking up 30-06 brass. Another option is 30-06 Cylindrical brass which you simply neck down and trim to length, this saves the step of having to neck the brass up for the calibers 348 and up.

The forming instructions earlier in this book explain the details of the reloading operation so it will not be repeated here.

I often run into shooters who want to use military brass because they have a ton of it and it's free. You can use it for Hawk cartridges but keep in mind the military brass is nearly always thicker than commercial brass so it will produce higher pressures if you use the same loads. So, be sure to reduce loads if you want to use military brass. You will probably get the same results with a little less powder, because pressure is directly correlated to velocity.

How to Form Brass for 338, 358, and 375 Hawk Calibers...

As with the smaller calibers earlier in this chapter, we recommend that you only use new unfired brass all from one manufacturers lot number when forming brass for Hawk Cartridges.

35 Whelen brass works best to form these cartridges (30-06 brass will work fine.) As a rule necking down two calibers or more works best to create a positive shoulder to head space against (sometimes referred to as a false shoulder as seen in Figure 1. above), i.e. 35 Whelen should be necked up to 411, so that it can then be necked back down to 358 Hawk. The new shoulder will be further forward, leaving a shorter neck, and creating a "false shoulder."

The first step is to use an oversized tapered expander ball to expand the neck of the cases to the larger size appropriate to your caliber. Install the expander ball on the decapping rod of the sizing die. Use plenty of case lube on the inside of the necks to make the process go easier (graphite lube will work). Expand the neck of the cases to the new oversize diameter. Be sure not to resize the neck at this point as this will unduly work the brass, as it comes back over the expander ball.

Now reinstall the correct size expander ball for the caliber you're loading on the decapping rod of the sizing die. Lube the outside of the cases for sizing as in normal reloading procedures.

Run the brass you just expanded through the size die. At this point you will want to have your rifle handy, check the cases for proper fit in the chamber of your rifle. The bolt should close on the brass without undue force, but you should feel the bolt drag slightly on the brass as the bolt closes. Once this setting is located lock your sizing die lock ring, using the set screw, to prevent the die from moving. Check each piece of sized brass for proper fit.

Congratulations, that is all there is to it.

Now just, prime, and load as usual, with the components of your choice, and fireform. You will want to trim to length after fireforming as the process will effect the neck length. Once the cases have been fireformed just reload as you would any factory caliber.

Trim length:
338 Hawk minimum length 2.465"
348 Hawk minimum length 2.460"
358 Hawk minimum length 2.450"
9.3mm Hawk minimum length 2.445"
375 Hawk minimum length 2.440"
Max length is .010" longer.

NOTE: Hawk Cartridges are true wildcats. It is <u>not</u> possible to fire any factory cartridge in a Hawk chamber. This will result in severe damage to your firearm and potential personal injury.

411 Hawk forming instructions...

Because the 411 Hawk shoulder area is relatively small it is unusually important that close attention is paid to headspace. The area of the shoulder is more than sufficient to headspace correctly, the concern is in fully fireforming the cartridge. The brass must make two sharp turns in a short distance at the shoulder. Brass is somewhat stiff, and has limited elasticity. So unless full pressure loads (55,000 PSI) are fired the shoulder will tend to be rounded and may not fully form to Hawk dimensions.

When forming 411 Hawk, you will need to expand the brass to .430". First use the tapered 411 expander ball to open the brass necks. Then install the .430" expander ball and expand the necks again. The results will look funny, the neck and shoulder area will be larger than the body of the case. Best results will come from expanding the case to .430" for about .750" from the mouth of the case. (To skip the above procedures use <u>cylinder 06 brass</u> and simply form the neck before fireforming.)

Fitting the brass to the chamber is slightly different with the 411. Run the brass through the 411 Hawk size die with the 411 expander installed. Size the neck down and set the shoulder height (headspace) so that when you close the bolt it requires some effort. It is necessary to leave the headspace longer than normal. This will insure the brass is held tightly against the breech face of the firearm, to properly form the brass.

Congratulations, that is all there is to it.

Now just, prime, and load as usual, with the components of your choice, and fireform. You will want to trim to length after fireforming as the process will effect the neck length. Once the cases have been fireformed just reload as you would any factory caliber. Suggested fireforming load, 63gr. H4895, 300gr. Hawk RN. This also happens to be a great hunting load. Light bullets and fast powders do not produce a long enough pressure curve to fully form the brass (experience is the best teacher).

Trim length for 411 Hawk, 2.420"	Max length is .010" longer.

ALWAYS WERE SAFETY GLASSES AND HEARING PROTECTION WHEN RELOADING OR SHOOTING.

If you are unfamiliar with the terminology and processes described here we recommend that you read any or all of the following; Nick Harvey's Practical Reloading Manual, Handbook for Shooters & Reloaders Vol. I & II by P.O. Ackley, Designing & Forming Custom Cartridges by Ken Howell, or just about any brand name reloading manual will contain the information you need to be a safe reloader.

240 Hawk

Heading out for an antelope or mule deer hunt in the wide open west? Well, the 240 Hawk is well suited for such trips, with a very long point blank range (see "Z Rule of 3").

The 240 Hawk is a cartridge for folks who love extreme velocity. Of course any twist rate that suits your needs can be used on the 240 Hawk. Contrary to the larger calibers in the Hawk line this cartridge is totally overbore. That's not necessarily a bad thing, it does mean that you can wring out unbelievable speed from this cartridge.

240 Hawk Chamber

Case capacity in the 240 Hawk is about 4% greater than the 240 Weatherby™, so you can use 240 Weatherby™ data as a starting point.

Headspace for the 240 thru the 3200 Hawk, what I call the small calibers, are all on the same headspace gage. They are formed from 280 Remington brass so the headspace is set up exactly the same way the 280 Ackley Improved is done, using the 280 Ackley Improved go gage is exactly what you want when headspacing "the small" caliber Hawk Caratridges.

The loads below were safe in our test guns but no two guns are alike, so use common sense and work up carefully, as you should with any load.

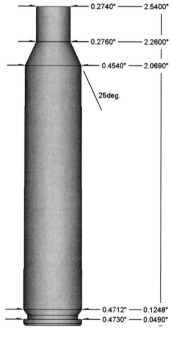

[Case Cap. 71.82 gr.]

Many groups in the .300" range were shot during testing. Prairie dogs and coyotes are in big trouble when this cartridge is around, or as a hunting buddy once said to me with just a hint of Western twang, "Now that's a flat shooter!"

Rifle/Barrel: Remington 700
Brass: R-P, 280 Remington
Barrel Length: 28"
Barrel Twist: 1-14 (special twist for light bullets)

Bullet Mfg	Bullet Wgt.	Style
Sierra	60	HP

Primer	Powder	Powder Wgt Gr.	Velocity FPS	Energy fp	Taylor KO Factor	Load OAL
CCI250	H380	51	3747	1870	7.80	2.940"
CCI250	H380	52	3892	2018	8.11	2.940"
CCI250	4831sc	57	3603	1729	6.07	2.940"
CCI250	4831sc	58.5	3733	1856	7.78	2.940"
CCI200	N150	50	3841	1965	8.00	2.965"
CCI200	N150	53	3968	2097	8.26	2.965"
CCI200	N550	50	3548	1677	7.39	2.965"
CCI200	N550	52	3744	1867	7.80	2.965"
CCI200	IMR4064	50	3550	1679	7.39	2.965"
CCI200	H4350	52	3550	1679	7.39	2.965"

Bullet Mfg	Bullet Wgt.	Style
Sierra	70	HPBT

Primer	Powder	Powder Wgt. Gr.	Velocity	Energy fp	Taylor KO Factor	Load OAL
CCI200	A2700	53	3600	2014	8.75	2.975"
CCI200	H4895	51	3900	2364	9.48	2.975"
CCI200	VARGET	48	3635	2053	8.83	2.975"

Bullet Mfg	Bullet Wgt.	Style
SPEER	70	TNT

Primer	Powder	Powder Wgt. Gr.	Velocity	Energy fp	Taylor KO Factor
Fed210	IMR4831	56.5	3638	2057	8.84
Fed210	RL15	57	3732	2165	9.07

Bullet Mfg	Bullet Wgt.	Style
SPEER	75	HP

Primer	Powder	Powder Wgt. Gr.	Velocity	Energy fp	Taylor KO Factor
CCI200	H4064	49	3652	2221	9.51
CCI200	RL15	49	3583	2138	9.33

Bullet Mfg	Bullet Wgt.	Style
NOSLER	80	BT

Primer	Powder	Powder Wgt gr.	Velocity	Energy fp	Taylor KO Factor
CCI200	W760	56	3625	2334	10.07
CCI200	RL-19	55	3447	2110	9.57
CCI200	H4320	49	3453	2118	9.59
CCI200	H414	54	3635	2347	10.09

Bullet Mfg	Bullet Wgt.	Style
Sierra	85	Spt

Primer	Powder	Powder Wgt.Gr.	Velocity	Energy fp	Taylor KO Factor
CCI200	RL 19	56	3451	2247	10.18
CCI200	H4831	52	3170	1896	9.35
CCI200	H4831	54	3300	2055	9.74
CCI200	H4831	55	3325	2086	9.81
Fed 210	IMR4350	56	3741	2641	11.04
Fed 210	IMR4350	56.5	3754	2659	11.08

Bullet Mfg	Bullet Wgt.	Style
HORNADY	87	Spt

Primer	Powder	Powder Wgt Gr.	Velocity	Energy fp	Taylor KO Factor
CCI200	H4350	57	3623	2535	10.94
CCI200	N160	56	3560	2448	10.75
CCI200	3100	54	3366	2188	10.17
CCI200	WIN748	51	3954	3020	11.94

Bullet Mfg	Bullet Wgt.	Style
NOSLER	100	Part

Primer	Powder	Powder Wgt. Gr.	Velocity	Energy fp	Taylor KO Factor
CCI200	RL 22	58	3420	2597	11.87
CCI200	H4831	55	3222	2305	11.18
CCI200	H4831	58	3480	2689	12.08
CCI200	BIGBOY	56	3115	2154	10.81

Bullet Mfg	Bullet Wgt.	Style
SPEER	105	Spt

Primer	Powder	Powder Wgt Gr.	Velocity	Energy fp	Taylor KO Factor
CCI200	BIGBOY	58	3358	2629	12.24
CCI200	BIGBOY	59	3662	3126	13.35
CCI200	RL 22	55	3159	2326	9.61
CCI200	RL 25	58	3260	2477	11.88

257 Hawk

The 257 Hawk is headspaced as a 280 Improved so you get a greater increase in case capacity that you would in a 25-06 Improved. Like it's smaller cousin the 240 Hawk this cartridge is built for those who, "Have a need for speed!"

P.O. Ackley did a lot of testing for cartridge design during his career and wrote that he personally preferred a 28 degree shoulder, believing that it delivered the best of all results for accuracy and brass life. He obviously sold what the public perceived as the "best", with his 40 degree shoulder designs. When I set out to design the smaller caliber Hawk cartridges I took Ackley's thoughts into consideration. By utilizing a 25 degree shoulder the brass is easy to form, delivers great case life, and accuracy. Also, a 25 degree shoulder is common to some factory cartridges these days, so it looks conventional to the shooter, making it more sexy looking than a 40 degree shoulder is.

257 Hawk Chamber

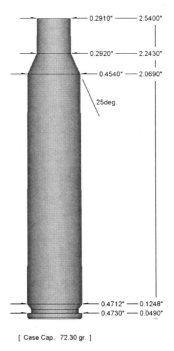

0.2910" —— 2.5400"

0.2920" —— 2.2430"

0.4540" —— 2.0690"

25deg.

0.4712" —— 0.1248"
0.4730" —— 0.0490"

[Case Cap. 72.30 gr.]

I have been asked why not used a sharper shoulder and get maximum case capacity. This is one of those gun writer created myths. The actual measured difference in capacity between a 25 degree shoulder and a 40 degree shoulder, all other dimensions being equal, is so small that it falls into the range of statistical variation, meaning there is not measurable velocity change.

When you're looking at cartridges that deliver maximum velocities for the bore diameter you should naturally leave questions like barrel life behind. Most of the clients who look at the 257 Hawk are thinking about a flat shooting deer or antelope cartridge, or maybe a long rang varminter. So, I always ask them to consider how many shots they will shoot from this rifle on an annual basis. For ninety percent of all hunters they suddenly realize that a barrel with a thousand rounds of top accuracy will easily last the rest of their life. For the other ten percent, they are the guys who will rebarrel the rifle by then anyway, so what the hell?

Rifle/Barrel: Douglas XX
Brass: R-P, 280 (Remington)
Barrel Length: 26"
Barrel Twist: 1-10

Bullet Mfg	Bullet Wgt.	Style
Sierra	75	Varminter

Primer	Powder	Powder Wgt. Gr.	Velocity	Energy fp	Taylor KO Factor	Load OAL
CCI200	H4064	48.1	3444	1975	9.5	3.125
CCI200	RL 15	47.0	3369	1890	9.3	3.125

Bullet Mfg	Bullet Wgt.	Style
Sierra	87	Sptz.

Primer	Powder	Powder Wgt. Gr.	Velocity	Energy fp	Taylor KO Factor	Load OAL
CCI200	H4350	56	3426	2267	10.9	3.135
CCI200	N160	55	3359	2180	10.7	3.135
CCI200	Win 748	50	3748	2714	12	3.135

Bullet Mfg	Bullet Wgt.	Style
Sierra	90	GameKing

Primer	Powder	Powder Wgt. Gr.	Velocity	Energy fp	Taylor KO Factor	Load OAL
CCI200	N160	53	3019	1821	10	3.150
CCI200	BigGame	53	3276	2145	10.8	3.150
CCI200	H4831SC	57	3801	2887	12.6	3.150

Bullet Mfg	Bullet Wgt.	Style
Sierra	100	Sptz.

Primer	Powder	Powder Wgt. Gr.	Velocity	Energy fp	Taylor KO Factor	Load OAL
CCI200	RL22	60	3489	2703	12.8	3.180
CCI200	N160	55	3252	2348	11.9	3.180
CCI200	N160	56	3316	2441	12.2	3.180
CCI200	H4831SC	61	3470	2674	12.7	3.180
CCI200	IMR4350	54	3279	2387	12.0	3.180

Bullet Mfg	Bullet Wgt.	Style
NOSLER	120	Part.

Primer	Powder	Powder Wgt. Gr.	Velocity	Energy fp	Taylor KO Factor	Load OAL
CCI200	N160	56	3365	3017	14.8	3.240
CCI200	IMR4831	59	3254	2821	14.3	3.240
CCI200	H870	64	2810	2104	12.4	3.240
CCI200	H4831	57	3123	2599	13.8	3.240

264 Hawk

It is truly amazing how many 6.5mm fans are out there. The 264 Hawk has attracted about as much attention from shooters as any of the Hawk cartridges. There is a good relationship between case capacity, bullet weight, and sectional density making it a great choice for hunting in open country. 264 Hawk brings these variables together in a way that no other cartridge really does.

264 Hawk Chamber

Moderate levels of recoil will help the shooter or hunter to become truly comfortable with a rifle. The 264 Hawk is an exceptional choice for shooters who want the velocities associated with magnums but not the recoil. Knowledgeable reloaders come to realize that the added powder required for a true magnum cartridge adds a substantial amount of recoil.

This cartridge has long range potential because of the bullets and velocities it serves up. The ballistic coefficient of the target bullets available in 6.5mm make it an exceptional choice your long range work. At the same time, with a mercury recoil reducer and a good recoil pad this can be a great cartridge for young shooters, ladies, recoil sensitive shooters, or anybody that likes an accurate cartridge.

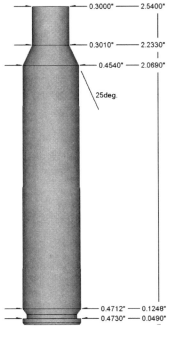

0.3000" — 2.5400"
0.3010" — 2.2330"
0.4540" — 2.0690"
25deg.
0.4712" — 0.1248"
0.4730" — 0.0490"

[Case Cap. 72.58 gr.]

Rifle/Barrel:	Winchester 70
Brass:	R-P, 280 Remington
Barrel Length:	26"
Barrel Twist:	1-14

Bullet Mfg	Bullet Wgt.	Style
Sierra	85	HP

Primer	Powder	Powder Wgt.gr.	Velocity	Energy fp	Taylor KO Factor	Load OAL
91/2M	H4895	50	3540	2365	11.35	3.155"
91/2M	IMR4350	55.5	3325	2086	10.66	3.150"
91/2M	W760	54	3385	2162	10.85	3.150"
91/2M	H414	57	3470	2272	11.12	3.150"

Bullet Mfg	Bullet Wgt.	Style
Hornady	95	VMax

Primer	Powder	Powder Wgt Gr.	Velocity	Energy fp	Taylor KO Factor	Load OAL
91/2M	H450	60	3500	2884	12.54	3.265"
91/2M	H4831SC	62	3500	2884	12.54	3.265"
91/2M	IMR4350	55	3310	2311	11.86	3.265"
91/2M	N160	57	3435	2489	12.31	3.265"

Bullet Mfg	Bullet Wgt.	Style
Sierra	100	HP

Primer	Powder	Powder Wgt. Gr.	Velocity	Energy fp	Taylor KO Factor	Load OAL
91/2M	N160	56	3280	2388	12.37	3.140"
91/2M	N160	57	3345	2484	12.62	3.140"

Note the difference in velocity just by changing the bullet. Bearing surface and ogive can effect ballistics more than you might guess.

Bullet Mfg	Bullet Wgt.	Style
Nosler	100	BT

Primer	Powder	Powder Wgt. Gr.	Velocity	Energy fp	Taylor KO Factor	Load OAL
91/2M	N160	56	3350	3488	17.69	3.240"
91/2M	N160	57	3440	3678	18.16	3.240"

Bullet Mfg	Bullet Wgt.	Style
Nosler	120	Bp

Primer	Powder	Powder Wgt. Gr.	Velocity	Energy fp	Taylor KO Factor	Load OAL
91/2M	N160	57	3440	3153	15.57	3.255"
91/2M	IMR4831	60	3330	2954	15.07	3.255"
91/2M	H870	65	2890	2225	13.08	3.255"
91/2M	H4831	58	3200	2728	14.48	3.255"

Bullet Mfg	Bullet Wgt.	Style
Sierra	140	MK

Primer	Powder	Powder Wgt.Gr.	Velocity	Energy fp	Taylor KO Factor	Load OAL
CCI220	IMR7828	54.5	2890	2596	15.26	3.250"
CCI220	IMR7828	55	2934	2676	15.49	3.250"
F215	IMR7828	54.5	2913	2637	15.38	3.250"
F215	IMR7828	55.5	2989	2777	15.78	3.250"
CCI200	N160	56	2962	2727	15.64	3.250"

Bullet Mfg	Bullet Wgt.	Style
Hornady	140	RN

Primer	Powder	Powder Wgt. Gr.	Velocity	Energy fp	Taylor KO Factor
CCI200	H4831	54.5	2810	2454	14.84
CCI200	H4831	55	2970	2742	15.68
CCI200	H4831SC	56	2925	2659	15.44
CCI200	IMR4350	52	2990	2779	15.79
CCI200	IMR4350	53	3090	2968	16.32
CCI200	R22	55	2926	2661	15.45
CCI200	R22	55.5	2955	2714	15.60
CCI200	IMR7828	54	2883	2583	15.22
CCI200	IMR7828	54.5	2923	2656	15.43
CCI200	IMR7828	55	2940	2687	15.52

270 Hawk

It's interesting to note that there are probably less wildcats in 270 caliber than almost any other bore diameter. P.O. Ackley was of the opinion that the 270 Winchester was about optimum for the 270 bore. Maybe this is the reason for the lack of wildcats in 270. Ackley was probably correct, however there are always shooters who want just a little more. The 270 Hawk delivers a little more, depending on the bullet you choose you can pick up as much as 150 to 200 feet per second over the 270 Winchester.

270 Hawk Chamber

Is this the absolute most you can get out of an 06 case in 270? Well, some would point to the 270 Gibbs as the max that can be squeezed from this family of cases. By comparing published data for the Gibbs with the data we have collected for the 270 Hawk it becomes obvious that the ballistic difference between the two cases is statistical at best. The Gibbs has the disadvantage of being harder to form, a sharp shoulder, and short neck; if these features delivered an advantage ballistically, yahoo! However, it provides absolutely no advantage so why compromise.

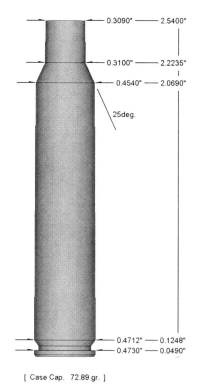

[Case Cap. 72.89 gr.]

I have a long time friend who is an avid reloader and shooter. When he heard I was getting a test gun together for the 270 Hawk he immediately volunteered to help. Because Doug Gregory keeps excellent records of his reloading I knew we could work together. A variety of powders were tested to see what might deliver the best velocities and H4350 turned up as the winner in that category.

The 270 Hawk is most readily formed from 280 Remington brass, simply neck size in a 270 Hawk die and fire form. Flat trajectory, low recoil, and great accuracy are the hallmarks of a good deer/antelope cartridge. The 270 Hawk has all of these, and provides the 270 fan with something new to play with.

Rifle/Barrel: 98 Mauser
Brass: R-P, 280 Remington
Barrel Length: 24"

Bullet Mfg	Bullet Wgt.	Style	Primer
Rem	130	Core-lokt	CCI 200

Powder	Powder Wgt. Gr.	Velocity	Energy fp	Taylor KO Factor
H414	55.5	3037	2662	15.6
H414	56	3080	2738	15.8
H4350	62	3345	3229	17.2
H4831	64	3168	2897	16.3
XMR3100	61	3043	2672	15.6
XMR3100	62	3105	2782	16
XMR3100	63	3145	2855	16.2
RL 22	63	3191	2939	16.4
IMR 4831	60	3179	2917	16.3

Bullet Mfg	Bullet Wgt.	Style	Primer
Hornady	140	BTSP	CCI 200

Powder	Powder Wgt. Gr.	Velocity	Energy fp	Taylor KO Factor
H4350	58	3161	3106	17.5
H4350	58.5	3214	3211	17.8
H4831	60.5	2997	2792	16.6

Bullet Mfg	Bullet Wgt.	Style	Primer
Winchester	150	Power Point	CCI 200

Powder	Powder Wgt. Gr.	Velocity	Energy fp	Taylor KO Factor
H4831	59.5	2885	2772	17.1
H4350	56	2982	2961	17.7
H4350	57	3051	3100	18.1
H4350	57.5	3054	3106	18.1

284 Hawk

This cartridge is very similar to the 280 Ackley Improved. The primary difference is the 25 degree shoulder, contrary to popular opinion that has virtually no effect on case capacity. Shoulder angle has more influence on feeding and case stretch.

Now that Nosler has brought the 280 Ackley Improved out as a SAAMI approved cartridge, wildcats like the 280 Hawk are a little less attractive. If you plan to use the Nosler brass for the 280 Ackley Improved for the Hawk you must recognize an important detail. When Nosler took the 280 Ackley Improved to SAAMI they changed the headspace from the traditional Ackley design. The Nosler brass therefore is .014" shorter than traditional.

Z-Hat Custom Inc. and Quality Cartridge have combined to offer correctly headstamped brass and loaded ammo for the 284 Hawk. With our brass there is no headspace issue to be concerned with.

The 284 Hawk cartridge is one of the best balanced of all the smaller caliber Hawk line (those between 240 and 3200). Versatility in loading is excellent, a wide variety of bullets are available and our test guns liked most anything we tried. This is a moderate recoil cartridge with plenty of velocity and power for most North American game with the possible exception moose

284 Hawk Chamber

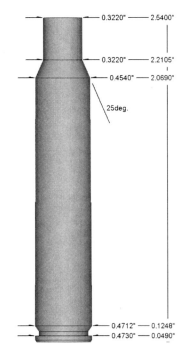

0.3220" —— 2.5400"

0.3220" —— 2.2105"

0.4540" —— 2.0690"

25deg.

0.4712" —— 0.1248"
0.4730" —— 0.0490"

[Case Cap. 73.34 gr.]

and brown bear. Velocities are close on the heals of the 7mm Remington Magnum, especially with lighter bullets that would be ideal for antelope or sheep hunting.

Rifle/Barrel: Winchester 70
Brass: R-P, 280 Remington
Barrel Length: 24"
Barrel Twist: 1-9.5"

Bullet Mfg	Bullet Wgt.	Style
Swift	150	Scirocco

Primer	Powder	Powder Wgt. Gr.	Velocity	Energy fp	Taylor KO Factor	Load OAL
WLR	RL 22	63	3115	3231	19	3.400
WLR	RL 25	65	2983	2963	18	3.430
WLR	RL 25	66	3031	3059	18	3.430

Bullet Mfg	Bullet Wgt.	Style
Hornady	154	SPTZ

Primer	Powder	Powder Wgt. Gr.	Velocity	Energy fp	Taylor KO Factor	Load OAL
WLR	RL 22	59	2827	2750	17	3.334
WLR	RL 22	61	2927	2948	18	3.334
WLR	RL 22	63	3003	3103	18	3.343

Bullet Mfg	Bullet Wgt.	Style
Sierra	160	Game King

Primer	Powder	Powder Wgt. Gr.	Velocity	Energy fp	Taylor KO Factor	Load OAL
WLR	RL 22	61	2905	2997	19	3.405
Win Mag	RL 22	60	2919	3026	19	3.405
Win Mag	RL 22	62	2986	3167	20	3.405
Win Mag	RL 25	64	2905	2998	19	3.405
Win Mag	RL 25	65	2986	3167	20	3.405

Bullet Mfg	Bullet Wgt.	Style
Nosler	160	Partition

Primer	Powder	Powder Wgt. Gr.	Velocity	Energy fp	Taylor KO Factor	Load OAL
WLR	RL 22	62	2989	3174	20	3.400
Win Mag	RL 22	61	3015	3229	20	3.405
WLR	RL 25	65	2976	3146	20	3.405
Win Mag	RL 25	65	2988	3172	20	3.405

Bullet Mfg	Bullet Wgt.	Style
Nosler	175 gr.	Partition

Primer	Powder	Powder Wgt. Gr.	Velocity	Energy fp	Taylor KO Factor	Load OAL
Win Mag	IMR 7828	59	2739	2914	19	3.400
Win Mag	IMR 7828	60	2801	3048	19	3.400
Win Mag	IMR 7828	61	2845	3145	20	3.400

300 Hawk

The first person outside our shop to test the 300 Hawk said it best, "It seems to shoot whatever I put through it!" This cartridge is well balanced and likes a wide variety of bullet/powder combinations. Test results have shown the 300 Hawk to be an accurate cartridge with near magnum performance and recoil very similar to the 30-06.

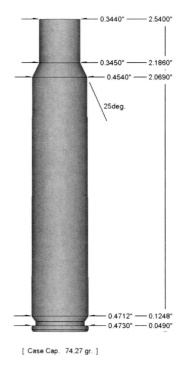

[Case Cap. 74.27 gr.]

If you could only have one rifle, this might well be it. There are a huge variety of bullets available for 30 calibers from every bullet maker. Loads from 100 to 250 grains, will allow you to take any game that comes your way.

The 30-06 case has been wildcatted in just about every way that you can imagine, and frankly in a few you would not want to imagine. What makes the 300 Hawk different if anything does is a couple of details that are often overlooked. First, like all the small caliber Hawk cartridges the parent case is the 280 Remington. This gives us a longer case with more case capacity than a 30-06 to begin with, then we improve the case. Second, it does not require overpressure to get results. The added case capacity takes care of that concern.

Rifle/Barrel: Remington 700
Brass: 280 Remington
Barrel Length: 22"
Barrel Twist: 1-10

Bullet Mfg	Bullet Wgt.	Style
Speer	150	Spt

Primer	Powder	Powder Wgt. Gr.	Velocity	Energy fp	Taylor KO Factor
CCI200	Varget	57	3095	3190	20.43
CCI200	H380	64	3198	3406	21.11
CCI200	IMR4895	56	3220	3453	21.25

Bullet Mfg	Bullet Wgt.	Style
Sierra	150	SP BT

Primer	Powder	Powder Wgt. Gr.	Velocity	Energy fp	Taylor KO Factor
CCI200	VARGET	56	3092	3184	20.41
CCI200	VARGET	57	3110	3221	20.53
CCI200	H380	63	3076	3151	20.30

Bullet Mfg	Bullet Wgt.	Style	Primer
Sierra	168	SP BT	CCI200

Powder	Powder Wgt. Gr.	Velocity	Energy fp	Taylor KO Factor
RL 19	63	3012	3384	22.26
IMR4320	55	2938	3219	21.73
H380	60	3032	3429	22.41
IMR4350	62	2928	3198	21.64
IMR4350	63	3108	3603	22.97
H4831sc	61	2676	2671	19.78
IMR4895	54	2706	2731	20.00
IMR4895	56	3019	3399	22.32
IMR4895	57	3061	3495	22.63
IMR4895	58	3092	3566	22.86

Bullet Mfg	Bullet Wgt.	Style
Sierra	180	SptBT

Primer	Powder	Powder Wgt. Gr.	Velocity	Energy fp	Taylor KO Factor
CCI200	IMR4350	60	2887	3331	22.87
CCI200	IMR4350	61	2938	3449	23.27

Bullet Mfg	Bullet Wgt.	Style
Sierra	200	SptBT

Primer	Powder	Powder Wgt. Gr.	Velocity	Energy fp	Taylor KO Factor
CCI200	IMR4350	56	2730	3309	24.02
CCI200	IMR4350	58	2801	3484	24.65

3200 Hawk

"What do you mean 3200?" Well, it's an 8mm that will push a 150 gr. bullet over 3200 feet per second. 8mm fans will love the 3200 Hawk. You're not stuck with a belted case or an antiquated military cartridge. Here is a modern design that will deliver respectable ballistics without unnecessary recoil.

Americans frequently overlook metric cartridges. 6mm and 7mm cartridges have gathered a following, but it took many years of positive reports and explanation of how they related to inch designation for that following to appear. 8mm is certainly one of the calibers that are ignored by Americans. They deliver more punch than a 30 caliber simply because of the larger diameter. Although bullet selection is limited there are still plenty of good projectiles for the hunter in 8mm.

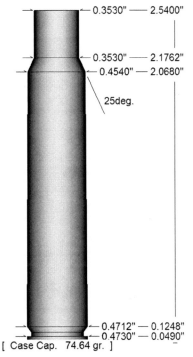

0.3530" —— 2.5400"

0.3530" —— 2.1762"
0.4540" —— 2.0680"

25deg.

0.4712" — 0.1248"
0.4730" — 0.0490"

[Case Cap. 74.64 gr.]

Here is a comment from one client who has a 3200 Hawk, *"Not only is it going almost as fast as 8mm Remington Mag. factory ballistics but I shot two 300 yard groups from a bench with this load. First group measured exactly 2 inches I was pretty happy, but my second group measured 1 and 3/4 inches for three shots each. Brass life with these loads has been super, as a matter of fact I am still using the same brass I started with a year ago and some have been reloaded 5+ times."* That says it all!

Brass: 280 Remington
Barrel Length: 22"
Barrel Twist: 1-10

Bullet Mfg	Bullet Wgt.	Style
Sierra	150	Spt

Primer	Powder	Powder Wgt. Gr.	Velocity	Energy fp	Taylor KO Factor
CCI200	H4895	59	3183	3374	22.03
CCI200	H4895	60	3233	3481	22.38
CCI200	RI 15	63	3201	3412	22.16

Bullet Mfg	Bullet Wgt.	Style
Remington	185	Spt

Primer	Powder	Powder Wgt. Gr.	Velocity	Energy fp	Taylor KO Factor
CCI200	H4350	62	2764	3138	23.59
CCI200	H4350	66.5	3015	3733	25.74

Bullet Mfg	Bullet Wgt.	Style
Speer	200	HC

Primer	Powder	Powder Wgt. Gr.	Velocity	Energy fp	Taylor KO Factor
CCI200	H4350	64	2840	3581	26.21

Bullet Mfg	Bullet Wgt.	Style
Sierra	220	SptBT

Primer	Powder	Powder Wgt. Gr.	Velocity	Energy fp	Taylor KO Factor
CCI200	RI 19	65	2718	3608	27.59
CCI200	H4350	61	2707	3579	27.48
CCI200	H4895	53.5	2703	3568	27.44
CCI200	RI 15	56	2707	3579	27.48
CCI200	H4350	62	2764	3731	28.06

338 Hawk

338 Hawk is headspaced with the same gage as the 348, 358, 9.3mm, 375, and 411 Hawk cartridges. By grouping the headspace gages I saved a lot of confusion for gunsmiths in the future. I consider this list to represent the "Big" Hawk Cartridges. The cartridges on this list <u>cannot</u> be fireformed from any factory ammo. Its necessary to form the brass first in a die to create these cartridges. See page 94 for details on forming Hawk brass.

This cartridge is one of my personal favorites, simply because I liked the 338-06 long before I started working on the Hawk line-up. I still have the first 338 Hawk that I chambered, it has taken game from Kodiak, Alaska to Casper, Wyoming. The 17 degree 30 minute shoulder makes it a smooth feeding hunting cartridge. I used the 230 grain Hawk bullet and it has never failed me.

338 Hawk Chamber

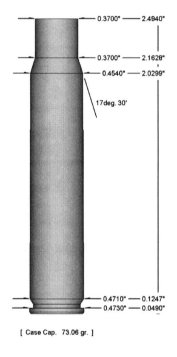

0.3700" —— 2.4940"

0.3700" —— 2.1628"
0.4540" —— 2.0299"

17deg. 30'

0.4710" —— 0.1247"
0.4730" —— 0.0490"

[Case Cap. 73.06 gr.]

On a historical note, the 338 Scovill appeared in an article just one month before the 338 Hawk. They say, "Great minds think alike, but fools seldom differ." I will let you decide how to apply that line. The 338 Scovill is identical to the 338 Hawk except for the shoulder angle and therefore it needs it's own dies and gages. However, you can interchange load data for the two cartridges.

Fred's 338 Hawk on Kodiak

If you're a fan of the 338-06 the 338 Hawk is a natural for you. With nearly 10% more capacity than a 338-06, ballistics of the 338 Hawk are what most 338-06 shooters wish they could get; A 230 grain bullet with the trajectory of a 180 gr. bullet from a 30-06.

If high velocity is your game the 338 Hawk can do that too, with a 180 grain bullet at over 2900 feet per second. The 338 Hawk is a highly versatile cartridge.

Rifle/Barrel: DOUGLAS
Brass: R-P 35 WHELEN
Barrel Length: 24"
Barrel Twist: 1-10

Bullet Mfg	Bullet Wgt.	Style
Nosler	180	BT

Primer	Powder	Powder Wgt. Gr.	Velocity	Energy fp	Taylor KO Factor	Pressure psi
CCI200	Imr4320	58.5	2911	3386	25.30	59,900
CCI200	Vv550	63	2924	3417	25.41	
CCI200	RI 15	60	2941	3456	25.56	60,000
CCI200	IMR4350	63	2800	3133	24.34	
CCI200	IMR4064	57.5	2887	3331	25.09	

Bullet Mfg	Bullet Wgt.	Style
NOSLER	200	BT

Primer	Powder	Powder Wgt. Gr.	Velocity	Energy fp	Taylor KO Factor	Load OAL
CCI200	RL 15	55	2760	3382	26.65	3.28"
CCI200	RL 15	58	2860	3632	27.62	3.28"
CCI200	VV N550	59	2831	3559	27.34	3.28"
CCI200	H 414	64	2781	3434	26.86	3.28"
CCI200	RL-19	69.5	2753	3365	26.59	3.28"
CCI200	IMR4064	55.2	2756	3373	26.62	3.28"

Bullet Mfg	Bullet Wgt.	Style
Hawk	200	RN

Primer	Powder	Powder Wgt. Gr.	Velocity	Energy fp	Taylor KO Factor
CCI200	H4895	55	2712	3266	26.19
CCI200	IMR4064	55	2862	3637	27.64

Bullet Mfg	Bullet Wgt.	Style
Speer	200	Spt

Primer	Powder	Powder Wgt. Gr.	Velocity	Energy fp	Taylor KO Factor	Pressure psi
CCI200	RL 15	58	2830	3556	27.33	59,700
CCI200	RL 15	58.5	2863	3639	27.56	
CCI200	H4350	65.5	2806	3496	27.10	
CCI200	H380	65	2778	3427	26.83	57,400

Bullet Mfg	Bullet Wgt.	Style
Nosler	210	Part.

Primer	Powder	Powder Wgt. Gr.	Velocity	Energy fp	Taylor KO Factor	Pressure psi
CCI200	AA 2700	61	2704	3409	27.42	
CCI200	IMR4320	65	2756	3541	27.95	
CCI200	RL15	57	2766	3567	28.05	
CCI200	RL15	58	2849	3784	28.89	59,900
CCI200	IMR4320	55	2630	3225	26.67	59,800
CCI200	H 380	64	2685	3361	27.23	58,000
BR2	H4895	53	2700	3399	27.38	
BR2	IMR4895	56.5	2778	3598	28.17	
BR2	IMR4064	56.5	2758	3546	27.97	
BR2	N135	55	2719	3447	27.57	
BR2	H414	65	2848	3782	28.88	

Bullet Mfg	Bullet Wgt.	Style
NOSLER	225	Part

Primer	Powder	Powder Wgt. Gr.	Velocity	Energy fp	Taylor KO Factor	Pressure psi
CCI200	Varget	59	2768	3827	30.07	
CCI200	VV N550	56	2520	3172	27.38	
CCI200	IMR4320	54	2560	3274	27.81	59,600

Bullet Mfg	Bullet Wgt.	Style
Hawk	230	RN

Primer	Powder	Powder Wgt. Gr.	Velocity	Energy fp	Taylor KO Factor	Load OAL
CCI200	IMR4320	55	2578	3394	28.63	3.24"
CCI200	H414	60	2615	3492	29.04	3.24"

Bullet Mfg	Bullet Wgt.	Style
SPEER	250	GS

Primer	Powder	Powder Wgt. Gr.	Velocity	Energy fp	Taylor KO Factor
CCI200	AA 2700	56.6	2440	3304	29.45
CCI200	AA 2700	57.8	2455	3345	29.64
CCI200	RL-19	62	2449	3329	29.56
CCI200	RL-19	63	2545	3595	30.72
CCI200	H4831SC	64	2473	3394	29.85
CCI200	IMR4320	52.5	2369	3186	29.92
CCI200	VV N550	56	2502	3474	30.20
CCI200	IMR4350	61	2497	3461	30.14

Rifle/Barrel: 338 HAWK / SHILEN
Brass: R-P 35 WHELEN
Barrel Length: 23"
Barrel Twist: 1-10

Bullet Mfg	Bullet Wgt.	Style
HORNADY	225	Spt

Primer	Powder	Powder Wgt. Gr.	Velocity	Energy fp	Taylor KO Factor	Pressure psi
CCI200	IMR4064	54.5	2588	3346	28.12	
CCI200	IMR4064	55.5	2592	3356	28.16	
CCI200	IMR4064	56	2700	3641	29.33	
CCI200	IMR4064	57	2745	3764	29.82	
CCI200	IMR4350	60	2435	2962	26.45	
CCI200	IMR4350	62.2	2650	3508	28.79	
CCI200	H380	63	2585	3338	28.08	59,200
CCI200	RL15	55.5	2585	3338	28.08	
CCI200	H4895	55	2726	3712	29.62	
CCI200	H4895	56	2759	3802	29.97	
CCI200	H335	53	2623	3473	28.50	
CCI200	H335	54	2646	3497	28.75	

Bullet Mfg	Bullet Wgt.	Style
HAWK	230	RN

Primer	Powder	Powder Wgt. Gr.	Velocity	Energy fp	Taylor KO Factor
CCI200	IMR4350	63	2591	3428	28.77
CCI200	IMR4350	64.5	2598	3446	28.85
CCI200	VARGET	58.5	2725	3792	30.26
CCI200	VARGET	60	2750	3862	30.54
CCI200	RI15	55.4	2560	3346	28.43
CCI200	RI15	58.3	2711	3753	30.11
CCI200	AA 2700	61.5	2615	3492	29.04

348 Hawk

The 348 Hawk was assembled for a client's request. Because of the limited bullet availability this would not have been a caliber I would have worked up without a client asking me. Because bullets are so limited in 348 caliber I would not recommend this caliber for that reason alone. Most of the bullets in this caliber are not designed for high velocity, so keep that in mind if you choose this cartridge.

However, it is certainly capable of taking any North American game, especially with good bullets like Hawk or Barnes. Since this is a cartridge likely used in a bolt gun, I would suggest using the Spitzer style bullets to get the best ballistics out of it.

348 Hawk Chamber

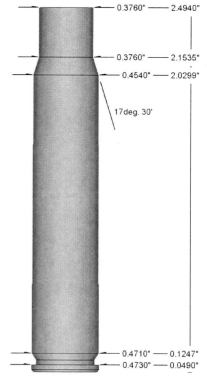

0.3760" —— 2.4940"

0.3760" —— 2.1535"
0.4540" —— 2.0299"

17deg. 30'

0.4710" —— 0.1247"
0.4730" —— 0.0490"

[Case Cap. 73.34 gr.]

Rifle/Barrel: Mauser Vz/24
Brass: R-P, 35 Whelen
Barrel Length: 26"
Barrel Twist: 1-14

Bullet Mfg	Bullet Wgt.	Style
Winchester	200	ST

Primer	Powder	Powder Wgt. Gr.	Velocity	Energy fp	Taylor KO Factor
CCI200	AA2700	64	2786	3446	27
CCI200	RL15	58	2865	3644	28
CCI200	H4350	65	2814	3516	27
CCI200	H380	64	2789	3454	27

Bullet Mfg	Bullet Wgt.	Style	Primer
Hawk	230	RN	CCI200

Powder	Powder Wgt. Gr.	Velocity	Energy fp	Taylor KO Factor	Load OAL
IMR4320	56	2660	3613	29	3.25"
H414	61	2704	3734	30	3.25"
RL-15	58	2734	3817	30	3.25"
H380	61.5	2568	3368	28	3.25"

Bullet Mfg	Bullet Wgt.	Style	Primer
Hawk	250	FBSPT	CCI200

Powder	Powder Wgt. Gr.	Velocity	Energy fp	Taylor KO Factor
N133	50	2399	3194	29
N140	57	2502	3474	31
Varget	58	2569	3663	31
H4895	56	2571	3669	31

Bullet Mfg	Bullet Wgt.	Style	Primer
Hawk	270	FBSPT	CCI200

Powder	Powder Wgt. Gr.	Velocity	Energy fp	Taylor KO Factor
N550	63	2493	3726	32
H4895	55	2458	3622	32
RL15	56	2464	3640	32

358 Hawk

In the beginning... there was the 338, 358, 375, and 411 Hawk.

So you might call the 358 one of the first-born cartridges in the Hawk line-up. If you're a fan of the 35 Whelen then you will love the 358 Hawk. The 358 Hawk safely delivers all the ballistics Whelen fans wish for at normal factory pressure levels.

358 Hawk Chamber

Anna Snapp likes Dad's
375 Hawk/Scovill

In 1995 Graydon Snapp walked into my shop in Casper, Wyoming. Graydon had read the article about the 375 Hawk, in Rifle Magazine #166. Being a fan of the 35 Whelen he was sure that a 358 Hawk would be the way to go. To make a long story short (the whole story is in Chapter 1), first we built Graydon a 375 Hawk/Scovill, which his daughter has since adopted. Graydon was so pleased with the results of his 375 Hawk that he decided the 358 Hawk (his first choice) was an absolute must. Here are some of the results of our tests.

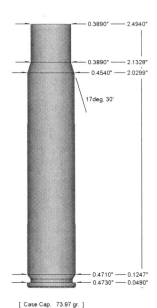

0.3890" —— 2.4940"

0.3890" —— 2.1328"
0.4540" —— 2.0299"

17deg. 30'

0.4710" —— 0.1247"
0.4730" —— 0.0490"

[Case Cap. 73.97 gr.]

Rifle/Barrel: Mauser Vz/24
Brass: R-P, 35 Wehlen
Barrel Length: 26"
Barrel Twist: 1-14
Pressure measured by: Oehler model 43.

Bullet Mfg	Bullet Wgt.	Style	Primer
North Fork	200	Protected Point	CCI200

Powder	Powder Wgt. Gr.	Velocity	Energy fp	Taylor KO Factor	Pressure psi	Load OAL
RL 15	58	2674	3175	27.35		3.275"
RL 15	59	2687	3233	27.48	44,700	
IMR4320	59	2754	3395	28.17	51,600	3.255"
H 380	56	2502	2780	25.59		3.280"
H 380	58	2580	2956	26.39		3.280"
H 380	60	2552	2918	26.10	43,800	

Bullet Mfg	Bullet Wgt.	Style
Hornady	200	SP

Primer	Powder	Powder Wgt. Gr.	Velocity	Energy fp	Taylor KO Factor
CCI200	AA2700	64	2719	3283	27.81
CCI200	AA2700	65	2857	3624	29.22

Bullet Mfg	Bullet Wgt.	Style	Primer
North Fork	225	PP	CCI200

Powder	Powder Wgt. Gr.	Velocity	Energy fp	Taylor KO Factor	Pressure psi	Load OAL
RL 15	57	2602	3382	29.94	49,300	3.305"
RL 15	61	2796	3936	32.17	61,600	3.205'
VVN133	49	2406	2896	27.69		3.600"
VVN133	55	2660	3563	30.61	60,700	3.300"

Bullet Mfg	Bullet Wgt.	Style	Primer
Hawk	225	RN	CCI200

Powder	Powder Wgt. Gr.	Velocity	Energy fp	Taylor KO Factor	Pressure psi	Load OAL
RL15	57	2590	3351	29.8		3.165"
RL15	58	2673	3601	30.76	54,400	
VVN530	52	2516	3162	28.95		3.200"
VVN530	54	2612	3408	30.06		
VVN530	55	2687	3639	30.92	58,500	3.165"

Bullet Mfg	Bullet Wgt.	Style	Primer
Nosler	225	BT	CCI220

Powder	Powder Wgt. Gr.	Velocity	Energy fp	Taylor KO Factor	Pressure psi	Load OAL
VVN133	50	2504	3132	28.81		3.325"
VVN133	53	2606	3415	29.99	58,500	3.325"
H380	60	2587	3343	29.77		3.325"
IMR4320	57	2762	3811	31.78		3.325"
RL15	59	2731	3723	31.41		3.325"

Bullet Mfg	Bullet Wgt.	Style	Primer
Hawk	250	RN	CCI220

Powder	Powder Wgt. Gr.	Velocity	Energy fp	Taylor KO Factor	Pressure psi	Load OAL
VVN133	48	2252	2815	28.79		3.150"
VVN133	51.5	2427	3269	31.03	57,300	
Varget	59	2598	3746	33	62,700	
VVN140	58	2529	3580	32.34	54,900	
VVN140	59	2669	3954	34	62,000	
H4895	57.2	2601	3788	33.26	59,300	
N530	50	2353	3073	30.08		3.245"

Bullet Mfg	Bullet Wgt.	Style	Primer
Speer	250	GS	CCI200

Powder	Powder Wgt. Gr.	Velocity	Energy fp	Taylor KO Factor	Pressure psi	Load OAL
VVN530	50	2344	3049	29.97		3.25"
VVN530	51	2412	3229	30.84		
VVN530	52.5	2490	3466	31.84	59,500	

Bullet Mfg	Bullet Wgt.	Style	Primer
North Fork	250	PP	CCl200

Powder	Powder Wgt. Gr.	Velocity	Energy fp	Taylor KO Factor	Pressure psi	Load OAL
H4895	50	2330	3013	29.79		3.300"
H4895	56	2549	3635	33.17	57,200	
RL15	57	2561	3640	32.74	56,100	
RL15	57	2577	3686	32.95		3.280"
RL15	58.5	2561	3640	32.74	56100	

Bullet Mfg	Bullet Wgt.	Style	Primer
Hornady	250	SPZ	CCl200

Powder	Powder Wgt. Gr.	Velocity	Energy fp	Taylor KO Factor
Varget	57	2554	3620	32.65
Varget	58	2585	3709	33.05
Varget	59	2614	3792	33.42
H4895	56	2581	3697	33.00
H4895	57	2630	3839	33.63

Bullet Mfg	Bullet Wgt.	Style	Primer
North Fork	270	PP	CCI 200

Powder	Powder Wgt. Gr.	Velocity	Energy fp	Taylor KO Factor	Pressure psi	Load OAL
N550	62	2439	3566	33		
N550	64	2566	3947	35	56,000	3.280
H4895	52	2352	3316	32		
H4895	54	2432	3546	33		
H4895	56	2478	3681	34		
RL-15	54	2364	3350	32		
RL-15	56	2443	3578	33		

Bullet Mfg	Bullet Wgt.	Style	Primer
Swift	280	A-Frame	CCI 200

Powder	Powder Wgt. Gr.	Velocity	Energy fp	Taylor KO Factor	Pressure psi	Load OAL
N550	61	2401	3583	34		
N550	61.5	2468	3786	35	56,100	3.275

9.3mm Hawk

The 9.3x62 is the grandfather of the Hawk line of cartridges in many ways. One of the things that has kept the venerable old 9.3x62 from becoming a popular cartridge in the United States is the fact that it is designated for low pressure loading under CIP standards. This means that the velocities it produces in factory loadings do not impress American shooters, who are used to higher velocities.

Secondary to these velocity short comings is the lack of variety in bullets available. Factory loadings are normally in a 286 grain bullet weight. The sad fact is that the 9.3x62 is an awesome cartridge with a small North American following. It's sometimes called the 30-06 of Africa.

Changes are in the wind, today American shooters have available to them a better selection of bullet weights from a variety of makers. With full power loads this is a powerful rifle in a standard length action.

Headspace for the Hawk line is longer than for the 9.3x62 by a wide margin. It is not possible to shoot

9.3 Hawk Chamber

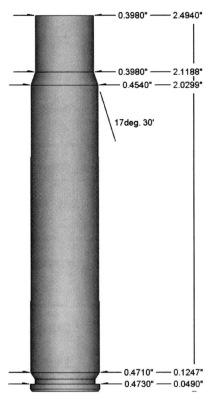

0.3980" —— 2.4940"

0.3980" —— 2.1188"
0.4540" —— 2.0299"

17deg. 30'

0.4710" —— 0.1247"
0.4730" —— 0.0490"

[Case Cap. 74.45 gr.]

144

9.3x62 brass in a Hawk chamber because of the headspace length and the diameter of the cases. The 9.3mm Hawk is based on the 30-06 case as are the 338, 348, 358, 375, and 411 Hawk.

Happily, this difference also allows us to run the pressures at the level of a modern cartridge. Especially since no old worn out firearm is chambered for the Hawk as might be the case with the 9.3x62. The 9.3 Hawk is a thoroughly modern cartridge that can take full advantage of modern powders for flat trajectories and incredible stopping power.

The 9.3 Hawk is a high pressure modern version of the old world favorite, 9.3x62.

Rifle/Barrel: Douglas XX
Brass: R-P, 35 Wehlen
Barrel Length: 24"
Barrel Twist: 1-14

Bullet Mfg	Bullet Wgt.	Style
Hawk	200	RN

Primer	Powder	Powder Wgt. Gr.	Velocity	Energy fp	Taylor KO Factor
WLR	H4895	61	2696	3228	28
WLR	IMR4320	61	2774	3417	29

Bullet Mfg	Bullet Wgt.	Style
Hawk	235	RN

Primer	Powder	Powder Wgt. Gr.	Velocity	Energy fp	Taylor KO Factor
WLR	H4895	61	2732	3844	33
WLR	AA2015	57	2730	3839	33
WLR	AA2495	58	2475	3155	30
WLR	RL15	60	2639	3587	32
WLR	RL12	58	2556	3365	31

Bullet Mfg	Bullet Wgt.	Style
Swift	250	AF

Primer	Powder	Powder Wgt. Gr.	Velocity	Energy fp	Taylor KO Factor
WLR	H4895	57	2510	3496	32
WLR	IMR4320	57	2640	3868	34
CCI200	Benchmark	56	2586	3711	33
CCI200	RL15	57	2463	3367	32

Bullet Mfg	Bullet Wgt.	Style
Hawk	250	RN

Primer	Powder	Powder Wgt. Gr.	Velocity	Energy fp	Taylor KO Factor
WLR	H4895	58	2651	3901	34
WLR	AA2015	56	2618	3804	34
WLR	AA2495	57	2354	3075	30
WLR	RL15	58	2489	3438	32
WLR	RL12	56	2365	3104	30
WLR	IMR4320	58	2636	3856	34
WLR	Varget	59	2687	4007	35
WLR	N140	59	2679	3934	34

Bullet Mfg	Bullet Wgt.	Style
GS Custom	270	FN

Primer	Powder	Powder Wgt. Gr.	Velocity	Energy fp	Taylor KO Factor
WLR	H4895	54	2398	3447	33
WLR	AA2495	55	2534	3849	35
WLR	RL15	56	2410	3481	34
WLR	RL12	54	2381	3398	33

Bullet Mfg	Bullet Wgt.	Style
Speer	270	SS

Primer	Powder	Powder Wgt. Gr.	Velocity	Energy fp	Taylor KO Factor
WLR	H4895	57	2512	3782	35
CCI200	AA2495	55	2402	3458	33
CCI200	RL15	57	2465	3642	34

Bullet Mfg	Bullet Wgt.	Style
Hawk	285	RN

Primer	Powder	Powder Wgt. Gr.	Velocity	Energy fp	Taylor KO Factor
WLR	H4895	56	2464	3841	36
WLR	RL12	54	2398	3638	35
WLR	RL15	56	2451	3801	36
WLR	IMR4320	55.5	2428	3730	36
WLR	AA2015	52.5	2417	3696	36
WLR	AA2495	54	2374	3566	35

Bullet Mfg	Bullet Wgt.	Style
Hornady	286	SPT

Primer	Powder	Powder Wgt. Gr.	Velocity	Energy fp	Taylor KO Factor
WLR	H4895	56	2458	3823	36
WLR	RL12	54	2393	3623	35
WLR	RL15	56	2444	3779	36
WLR	IMR4320	55.5	2417	3696	36

Bullet Mfg	Bullet Wgt.	Style
Swift	300	AF

Primer	Powder	Powder Wgt. Gr.	Velocity	Energy fp	Taylor KO Factor	Load OAL
WLR	H4895	55	2385	3788	37	3.195
WLR	RL15	55	2397	3827	37	
WLR	IMR4320	54	2346	3665	36	
WLR	AA2015	52.5	2380	3773	37	
WLR	AA2495	54	2358	3703	36	
CCI200	BL-C2	56	2348	3672	36	

375 Hawk/Scovill

The 375 Hawk was
the first cartridge in
this highly successful
group of cartridges. It
was in the latter part
of 1988 when Bob
Fulton, designer of
renowned HAWK
Bullets, had the idea
to build a rifle that
was suitable for
dangerous game, as
well as anything in
North American.
Recoil was another
major factor, Bob
wanted an 8 pound
rifle that would not
beat him up. A friend
gave Bob a rifle
chambered in 375
Whelen Improved.
Bob was not
impressed with the
mediocre ballistics.
So he started looking
for a better cartridge
design, based on the 30-06 case.

375 Hawk/Scovill Chamber

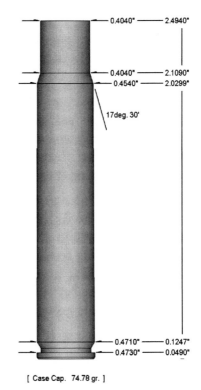

0.4040" ———— 2.4940"

0.4040" ———— 2.1090"
0.4540" ———— 2.0299"

17deg. 30'

0.4710" ———— 0.1247"
0.4730" ———— 0.0490"

[Case Cap. 74.78 gr.]

With Bob's long background in guns he had seen and shot many
wildcats. He was aware of the Gibbs line of cartridges, but the
goal was not to wring every last foot per second out of the 06
case. Rather, to have a reliable feeder and make the most
efficient use of it. Considerations of the design were weight,
cost, brass availability, low cost brass, low recoil and muzzle

blast, and easy conversion of any 06 size action. Bob wanted a case that is easy to form as well.

So Bob decided to use the basic design of the 9.3x62. By moving the shoulder forward and straitening the body taper, Bob managed to increase the powder capacity of the venerable old 30-06 cartridge by a total of 9% over the original design. He used the original 17 degree shoulder angle to facilitate reliable feeding.

When Bob went to the range with is new gun and a chronograph he was pleasantly surprised. His original goal was to increase velocity to 2600 fps with a 250 gr. bullet. Bob discovered that he could easily surpass his original goal with a wide margin for safety. In reality he achieved 2700 fps with a 250gr. bullet.

Bob took his gun to Dave Scovill, editor for Rifle and Handloader Magazines. Dave liked the 375 Hawk so much that he subsequently had two rifles made in the caliber. Dave changed the dimensions for his guns to North American standards for the 30-06 case. When his dies came from the maker they were marked 375 Scovill.

Bob Fulton had always used 30-06 brass for his 375 Hawk with no difficulty. The difference in dimensions serves an important purpose Bob explains, "The 9.3x62 follows the standard British practice of slightly looser chambering for use in Africa and other hot climates. That improves reliability of extraction, the extra room in the chamber is there to take advantage of the way that brass stretches and contracts."

Dave noted that use of a 9.3 reamer and 06 brass left a slight bulge on the case at the web, he cited concerns about stretching and possible head separations as the reason for using the smaller 06 case dimensions for his version of the 375 Hawk. *Editors Note: There is only one cause of case head separations, excessive headspace, this is axiomatic to gunsmithing.*

Ballistically the two versions are identical although ammunition cannot be interchanged. This cartridge is so popular that Barnes included it in their reloading manual and RCBS has made it a standard group G die.

When it comes to hunting with the 375 Hawk, I will always remember a hunt with Graydon Snapp. We were just south of Buffalo Wyoming on a friend of my Dad's ranch. Graydon and I were hiking along a branch of Crazy Woman Creek in midday, this would often push up Mule Deer from the tall grass that lined the creek banks. Several deer jumped up and a huge doe (any deer area) stopped just over a hundred yards from us on a flat along the hillside. Graydon dumped her with one shot and we made our way up the hill.

I walked straight to the doe. Graydon walked to where she had been standing when he shot, he looked around as if looking for the blood trail, then glanced my way with a smile and said, "Now that's my kind of a blood trail!" I was standing about three yards from Graydon where his doe was laying.

Special thanks to Mike Brady, founder of North Fork Bullets for his contributions to the pressure data provided here. Data was collected using an Oehler Model 43, the data was accurate for the rifle tested, many variables can change results, your results may vary, so, work up loads carefully.

Rifle/Barrel: Mauser 98
Brass: R-P, 35 Wehlen
Barrel Length: 24"
Barrel Twist: 1-12

Throat: Original length Clymer reamer
This throating works well for 1895 Wincheser or Browning lever actions.

Bullet Mfg	Bullet Wgt.	Style	Primer
Hornady	225	SP	CCI 200

Powder	Powder Wgt. Gr.	Velocity	Energy fp	Taylor KO Factor	Pressure psi	Load OAL
IMR3031	51	2309	2853	27.83	34,100	3.200
Benchmark	57.3	2673	3569	32.22	52,200	3.200
Benchmark	58.8	2771	3836	33.40	58,400	3.200
H335	60.3	2738	3745	33.00	59,700	3.200
H4895	58.6	2637	3474	31.79	45,400	3.200
H4895	61.7	2737	3742	32.99	52,200	3.200

Bullet Mfg	Bullet Wgt.	Style	Primer
Swift	250	A-Frame	CCI200

Powder	Powder Wgt. Gr.	Velocity	Energy fp	Taylor KO Factor	Pressure psi	Load OAL
H4895	57.7	2606	3769	34.90	60,100	3.110

154

Bullet Mfg	Bullet Wgt.	Style	Primer
North Fork	250	PP	CCI 200

Powder	Powder Wgt. Gr.	Velocity	Energy fp	Taylor KO Factor	Pressure psi	Load OAL
H4895	59	2637	3859	35.32	56,400	3.150
H4895	60	2646	3886	35.44	58,100	3.180
RL15	57.6	2522	3530	33.78	50,300	3.150

Bullet Mfg	Bullet Wgt.	Style	Primer
Sierra	250	SPBT	CCI200

Powder	Powder Wgt. Gr.	Velocity	Energy fp	Taylor KO Factor	Pressure psi	Load OAL
H4895	58.6	2664	3939	35.68	62,500	3.200

Bullet Mfg	Bullet Wgt.	Style	Primer
Swift	270	A-Frame	CCI200

Powder	Powder Wgt. Gr.	Velocity	Energy fp	Taylor KO Factor	Pressure psi	Load OAL
H414	59.5	2295	3157	33.20	53,200	3.100
H414	61.4	2366	3356	34.22	58,000	3.100

Bullet Mfg	Bullet Wgt.	Style	Primer
North Fork	270	PP	CCI200

Powder	Powder Wgt. Gr.	Velocity	Energy fp	Taylor KO Factor	Pressure psi	Load OAL
H4895	55	2410	3481	34.85	49,300	3.150
H4895	57	2471	3660	35.74	52,600	3.150

Bullet Mfg	Bullet Wgt.	Style	Primer
North Fork	300	PP	CCl200

Powder	Powder Wgt. Gr.	Velocity	Energy fp	Taylor KO Factor	Pressure psi	Load OAL
H4895	54.7	2352	3684	37.80	58,600	3.175
BL-C2	54	2259	3399	36.31	52,600	3.150
BL-C2	57	2358	3703	37.90	59,300	3.150

Below loads were tested with a lengthened throat to take better advantage of magazine length in bolt actions (.175" longer than Clymer chamber reamer).

Bullet Mfg	Bullet Wgt.	Style	Primer
Hornady	225	SPT	CCl200

Powder	Powder Wgt. Gr.	Velocity	Energy fp	Taylor KO Factor	Pressure psi	Load OAL
Benchmark	59	2757	3797	33.23	53,900	3.170
Benchmark	60.5	2798	3911	33.73	56,200	3.170

Bullet Mfg	Bullet Wgt.	Style	Primer
SPEER	235	SPT	CCI200

Powder	Powder Wgt. Gr.	Velocity	Energy fp	Taylor KO Factor	Pressure psi	Load OAL
Benchmark	58	2675	3733	33.68	51,300	3.200
Benchmark	59.5	2721	3863	34.26	54,500	3.200
Benchmark	60	2772	4009	34.90	60,400	3.200

Bullet Mfg	Bullet Wgt.	Style	Primer
Hawk	250	SPT	CCI200

Powder	Powder Wgt. Gr.	Velocity	Energy fp	Taylor KO Factor	Pressure psi	Load OAL
IMR4320	59	2583	3703	34.59	53,900	3.270
IMR4320	60.5	2649	3895	35.48	60,600	3.270
H4895	59	2669	3954	35.75	59,100	3.270
H4895	60	2736	4155	36.64	*63,000	3.270

* = Exceeds safe pressures, reference only!

Bullet Mfg	Bullet Wgt.	Style	Primer
SWIFT	250	SPT	CCI200

Powder	Powder Wgt. Gr.	Velocity	Energy fp	Taylor KO Factor	Pressure psi	Load OAL
IMR4320	61	2623	3819	35.13	55,200	3.180

Bullet Mfg	Bullet Wgt.	Style	Primer
North Fork	250	PP	CCI200

Powder	Powder Wgt. Gr.	Velocity	Energy fp	Taylor KO Factor	Pressure psi	Load OAL
BenchMark	56	2538	3575	33.99	55,200	3.270
BenchMark	57	2605	3766	34.89	59,000	3.270
RL15	57.6	2493	3449	33.39	44,300	3.270
RL15	59.7	2657	3918	35.58	55,600	3.270
Varget	59	2540	3581	34.02	51,900	3.270
IMR4320	61.5	2636	3857	35.30	57,100	3.270
H4895	60.5	2660	3927	35.63	55,800	3.270
H4895	61.5	2695	4031	36.09	58,400	3.270

Bullet Mfg	Bullet Wgt.	Style	Primer
North Fork	270	PP	CCI200

Powder	Powder Wgt. Gr.	Velocity	Energy fp	Taylor KO Factor	Pressure psi	Load OAL
RE15	57	2510	3776	36.31	57,300	3.270
IMR4320	58	2491	3719	36.03	52,600	3.210
IMR4320	59	2496	3734	36.10	53,200	3.210
IMR4320	60.5	2575	3975	37.25	57,700	3.260
IMR4320	61	2592	4027	37.49	61,700	3.265
N140	56	2356	3327	34.08	45,400	3.270
N140	60	2487	3708	35.97	52,900	3.270
N140	62	2553	3907	36.93	58,200	3.265
H4895	58	2539	3864	36.72	59,300	3.270

Bullet Mfg	Bullet Wgt.	Style	Primer
North Fork	300	PP	CCI200

Powder	Powder Wgt. Gr.	Velocity	Energy fp	Taylor KO Factor	Pressure psi	Load OAL
RE15	55.0	2332	3622	37.48	52,600	3.285
RE15	57	2367	3732	38.04	54,300	3.270
BL-C2	57	2377	3763	38.20	61,000	3.270
Varget	56	2276	3450	36.58	52,600	3.270
IMR4320	57	2375	3757	38.17	57,100	3.270
IMR4320	57.5	2383	3782	38.30	56,700	3.270
H4895	55.5	2376	3760	38.19	59,000	3.270

Bullet Mfg	Bullet Wgt.	Style	Primer
SWIFT	300	SPT	CCI 200

Powder	Powder Wgt. Gr.	Velocity	Energy fp	Taylor KO Factor	Pressure psi	Load OAL
IMR4320	57	2358	3703	37.90	56,100	3.200

411 Hawk

The 411 Hawk was the fourth cartridge of the Hawk line to be designed & tested. It was a direct result of the experiments that Graydon Snapp and I did with the 338 and 358 Hawk.

If a necked down 375 Hawk case worked well, why not a necked up version. Testing proved that a .411 bullet worked, but the small increase to a .416 will not work.

Setting the headspace of the brass for a 411 Hawk in your chamber requires more attention to detail than most cartridges. Your working with a small contact area for headspace as compared to the average cartridge. All that is required is good loading practices and a full reading of the brass forming instructions in this manual.

The 411 Hawk has been chambered in more custom

411 Hawk Chamber

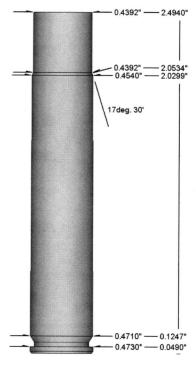

0.4392" — 2.4940"

0.4392" — 2.0534"
0.4540" — 2.0299"

17deg. 30'

0.4710" — 0.1247"
0.4730" — 0.0490"

[Case Cap. 77.03 gr.]

rifles than any of the other cartridges in the Hawk line. Years of success in the field, is the best testimony to the value of the now tried and true, 411 Hawk.

162

Rifle/Barrel: Douglas XX Premium
Brass: Z-Hat, .411 Hawk
Barrel Length: 25"
Barrel Twist: 1-20
Pressure by: Oehler Model 43.

Bullet Mfg	Bullet Wgt.	Style	Primer
North Fork	300	Protected Point (PP)	CCI200

Powder	Powder Wgt. Gr.	Velocity	Energy fp	Taylor KO Factor	Pressure psi	Load OAL
Benchmark	55.1	2241	3377	39.50	42,500	3.245"
Acc 2015	56	2239	3372	39.40	45,700	3.245"
Acc 2230	63	2608	4530	45.00	60,600	3.250"
VV-130	54.1	2413	3913	42.50	62,700	3.245"

Bullet Mfg	Bullet Wgt.	Style	Primer
Hawk	300	RN	CCI200

Powder	Powder Wgt. Gr.	Velocity	Energy fp	Taylor KO Factor	Pressure psi	Load OAL
VV-130	54.1	2427	3958	42.70	55,300	3.100"
VV-130	56	2475	4116	43.60	60,600	3.100"
Benchmark	57	2334	3666	41.10	47,500	3.100"
Benchmark	59.8	2491	4172	43.90	58,200	3.100"
Acc2015	56	2324	3631	40.90	50,000	3.100"
H4895	62	2505	4179	44.10		3.100"
H4895	63	2516	4216	44.30	57,200	3.100"
H4895	63.5	2530	4263	44.60		3.100"
H4895	64	2553	4341	45.00		3.100"
IMR4895	64.5	2515	4213	44.30		3.100"
BLC-2	59	2104	2948	37.10		3.100"
BLC-2	60	2244	3354	39.50		3.100"
BLC-2	63	2326	3603	41.00		3.100"
BLC-2	64	2371	3744	41.80		3.100"
IMR3031	56.5	2332	3622	41.10		3.100"
IMR3031	57.5	2350	3678	41.40		3.100"

Bullet Mfg	Bullet Wgt.	Style	Primer
North Fork	300	Protected Point (PP)	Fed 215

Powder	Powder Wgt. Gr.	Velocity	Energy fp	Taylor KO Factor	Pressure psi	Load OAL
BLC-2	70	2549	4366	44.90	51,900	3.245"
BLC-2	69	2533	4310	44.60		3.245"
BLC-2	69.5	2556	4390	45.00	54,000	3.245"

Bullet Mfg	Bullet Wgt.	Style	Primer
North Fork	325 Gr.	PP	Fed210

Powder	Powder Wgt. Gr.	Velocity	Energy fp	Taylor KO Factor	Pressure psi	Load OAL
H4895	61	2351	4020	44.86	50,700	3.250"
H4895	62	2376	4104	45.34	52,800	3.250"
H4895	63	2419	4255	46.16	57,200	3.250"
H4895	64	2479	4473	47.30	56,200	3.250"

Bullet Mfg	Bullet Wgt.	Style	Primer
North Fork	325 Gr.	PP	CCI200

Powder	Powder Wgt. Gr.	Velocity	Energy fp	Taylor KO Factor	Pressure psi	Load OAL
Acc2015	56	2198	3518	41.94	48,300	3.250"
Benchmark	55.1	2208	3552	42.13	46,900	3.250"
BLC-2	65.5	2401	4194	45.82	53,100	3.250"
H4895	63	2430	4261	46.37	57,000	3.250"

Bullet Mfg	Bullet Wgt.	Style	Primer
North Fork	325 Gr.	PP	Fed 215

Powder	Powder Wgt. Gr.	Velocity	Energy fp	Taylor KO Factor	Pressure psi	Load OAL
BLC-2	65.5	2387	4146	45.55	49,400	3.250"
BLC-2	66	2411	4232	46.01	52,200	3.250"

Bullet Mfg	Bullet Wgt.	Style	Primer
Swift	350	Spt	CCI200

Powder	Powder Wgt. Gr.	Velocity	Energy fp	Taylor KO Factor	Pressure psi	Load OAL
IMR4064	58	2128	3519	43.7		3.250"
IMR4064	59	2295	4093	47.2		3.250"
IMR4064	61	2366	4350	48.6		3.250"

Bullet Mfg	Bullet Wgt.	Style	Primer
North Fork	360	PP	CCI200

Powder	Powder Wgt. Gr.	Velocity	Energy fp	Taylor KO Factor	Pressure psi	Load OAL
BLC-2	61	2194	3848	46	51,100	3.250"
AA 2230	54	2188	3827	46	51,400	3.250"
AA 2230	57	2281	4159	48	56,700	3.250"
Varget	57	2181	3802	46	51,400	3.250"
H4895	56	2167	3754	45	51,800	3.250"

Bullet Mfg	Bullet Wgt.	Style	Primer
Hawk	400	RN	CCl200

Powder	Powder Wgt. Gr.	Velocity	Energy fp	Taylor KO Factor	Pressure psi	Load OAL
VV130	42.7	1829	3002	43.0	57,300	3.215"
R 15	57	2159	4172	50.7	58,700	3.280"

Rifle/Barrel: Ruger M-77
Brass: Rem. 35 Whelen
Barrel Length: 24"
Barrel Twist: 1-20

Bullet Mfg	Bullet Wgt.	Style	Primer
Sierra	170	Pistol	Win LR

Powder	Powder Wgt. Gr.	Velocity	Energy fp	Taylor KO Factor	Load OAL
IMR4198	64	3195	3853	31.19	2.850"

Bullet Mfg	Bullet Wgt.	Style	Primer
Remington	210	Pistol	Win LR

Powder	Powder Wgt. Gr.	Velocity	Energy fp	Taylor KO Factor	Load OAL
AA5744	50	2690	3374	33.2	2.900"
AA5744	52	2720	3449	33.5	2.900"
IMR4198	50	2650	3274	32.7	2.900"
IMR4198	54	2760	3551	34.0	2.900"
IMR4198	56	2860	3813	35.3	2.900"
IMR4198	62	2960	4085	36.5	2.900"

Bullet Mfg	Bullet Wgt.	Style	Primer
Barnes	350	Solid	Win LR

Powder	Powder Wgt. Gr.	Velocity	Energy fp	Taylor KO Factor	Load OAL
X-Terminator	58	2210	3795	45.4	3.410"
X-Terminator	60	2295	4093	47.2	3.410"
X-Terminator	62	2300	4110	47.3	3.410"
X-Terminator	64	2415	4532	49.6	3.410"

Bullet Mfg	Bullet Wgt.	Style	Primer
Hawk	350	RN	Win LR

Powder	Powder Wgt. Gr.	Velocity	Energy fp	Taylor KO Factor	Load OAL
AA2520	64	2170	3659	44.6	3.325"
AA2520	65	2220	3829	45.6	3.325"
AA2520	66	2235	3881	45.9	3.325"
AA2520	67	2280	4039	46.9	3.325"
AA2520	68	2365	4346	48.6	3.325"
AA2520	69	2410	4513	49.5	3.325"
TAC	54	2150	3592	44.2	3.325"
TAC	56	2195	3744	45.1	3.325"
TAC	58	2260	3969	46.4	3.325"
TAC	60	2290	4075	47.1	3.325"
TAC	62	2345	4273	48.2	3.325"

Bullet Mfg	Bullet Wgt.	Style	Primer
Barnes	350	X	Win LR

Powder	Powder Wgt. Gr.	Velocity	Energy fp	Taylor KO Factor	Load OAL
X-Terminator	61	2220	3829	45.6	3.410"
X-Terminator	62	2235	3881	45.9	3.410"
X-Terminator	63	2305	4128	47.4	3.410"
TAC	61	2135	3542	43.9	3.410"
TAC	62	2150	3592	44.2	3.410"
TAC	63	2190	3727	45.0	3.410"
TAC	64	2220	3829	45.6	3.410"
TAC	65	2340	4255	48.1	3.410"

Bullet Mfg	Bullet Wgt.	Style	Primer
Hawk	400	RN	Win LR

Powder	Powder Wgt. Gr.	Velocity	Energy fp	Taylor KO Factor	Load OAL
RL15	57	2150	4105	50.5	3.410"
RL15	58	2125	4010	49.9	3.410"
RL15	59	2175	4201	51.1	3.410"
AA2520	59	2020	3624	47.4	3.410"
AA2520	60	2040	3696	47.9	3.410"
AA2520	61	2080	3842	48.9	3.410"

Bullet Mfg	Bullet Wgt.	Style	Primer
Hawk	400	RN	Win LR

Powder	Powder Wgt. Gr.	Velocity	Energy fp	Taylor KO Factor	Load OAL
AA2520	62	2115	3972	49.7	3.410"
AA2520	63	2150	4105	50.5	3.410"
Big Game	62	2135	4048	50.1	3.410"
Big Game	64	2150	4105	50.5	3.410"

Bullet Mfg	Bullet Wgt.	Style
Hornady	400	SP

Primer	Powder	Powder Wgt. Gr.	Velocity	Energy fp	Taylor KO Factor	Load OAL
Win LR	RL15	56	2060	3768	48.40	3.340"
Win LR	RL15	58	2100	3916	49.30	3.340"
CCI200	RL15	59	2144	4082	50.97	3.340"

Lead Bullet Loads for the 411 Hawk

Bullet Wgt.	Style	Primer
270	RN	CCI200

Powder	Powder Wgt. Gr.	Velocity	Energy fp	Taylor KO Factor	Load OAL
IMR4198	35	1685	1702	26	2.950"
IMR4198	36	1760	1857	27	2.950"
IMR4198	37	1800	1942	28	2.950"
IMR4198	38	1830	2007	29	2.950"
IMR4198	39	2076	2583	32	2.950"
IMR3031	42	1820	1986	28	2.950"
IMR3031	44	1910	2187	30	2.950"
IMR3031	**40	1810	1964	28	2.950"
IMR3031	**42	1890	2141	29	2.950"

** same as above with magnum rifle primers

Lead Bullet Loads for the 411 Hawk continued...

Bullet Wgt.	Style	Primer
270	RN	CCI200

Powder	Powder Wgt. Gr.	Velocity	Energy fp	Taylor KO Factor	Load OAL
H4895	40	1600	1535	25	2.99"
H4895	42	1620	1573	25	2.99"
H4895	46	1850	2052	29	2.99"

411 Express

411 Express came about because of the availability of cylinder 06 brass that measures 2.650" in length. It seems logical that if the 411 Hawk performs well, but runs out of fuel capacity... a longer case would add capacity and therefore allow for more versatility. In truth the added capacity is not much help. Since this cartridge like the 411 Hawk is essentially a cylinder with very little shoulder there is no restriction to force the powder to burn in the chamber. Consequently, the powder burns the same in the 411 Express as it does in the 411 Hawk and added powder gains very little. So, ballistics of the 411 Express closely mirror the 411 Hawk.

Testing had shown that ball powders seemed to have the best chance of delivering more velocity with added capacity. When we tested that idea all we found was increased pressure with no real increase in velocity. This was particularly true with 400 grain bullets, where we thought we might get the best improvement.

Bottom line, the 411 Express offers no real gain came from it's added capacity and length. Most likely because of the case shape, if body diameter were increased noticeably then the increase in velocity would be better. But, that would be a totally different cartridge.

411 Express Chamber

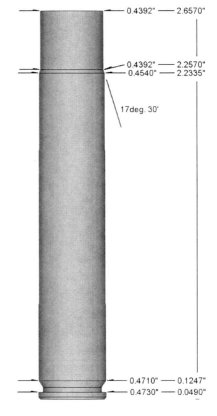

0.4392" —— 2.6570"

0.4392" —— 2.2570"
0.4540" —— 2.2335"

17deg. 30'

0.4710" —— 0.1247"
0.4730" —— 0.0490"

[Case Cap. 82.54 gr.]

Index

L to R: 240 Hawk, 257 Hawk, 264 Hawk, 270 Hawk, 284 Hawk, 300 Hawk, 3200 Hawk, and 30-06. Photo by www.mountainsunphotoart.com

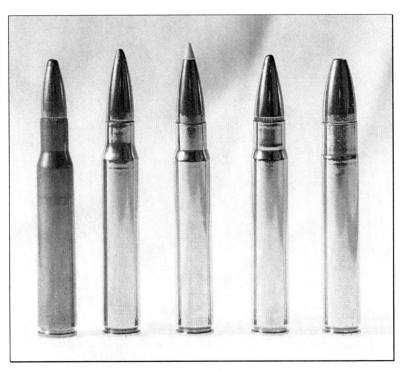

L to R: 30-06, 338 Hawk, 358 Hawk, 375 Hawk/S, 411 Hawk.

ALWAYS WERE SAFETY GLASSES AND HEARING
PROTECTION WHEN RELOADING OR SHOOTING.

If you are unfamiliar with the terminology and processes described here you are responsible to learn more. Do research, understand terminology, and think; your brain is the best safety device available.

The author and publishers of this book are not responsible for the use or misuse of it's contents by any individual or group. Utilize safe loading practices. Always start low and work up loads. Just because the loads published here were safe in test guns does not mean they will be safe in any other gun.

CPSIA information can be obtained at www.ICGtesting.com
Printed in the USA
267390BV00003B/2/P

9 780983 159803